Lord,

Thanks For The Journey

Lord, Thanks for the Journey

Trilogy Christian Publishers

A Wholly Owned Subsidiary of Trinity Broadcasting Network

2442 Michelle Drive

Tustin, CA 92780

10 9 8 7 6 5 4 3 2 1

Library of Congress Cataloging-in-Publication Data is available.

ISBN: 978-1-68556-202-1

ISBN: 978-1-68556-203-8

It is difficult sometimes to declare exactly when or where you began a journey. We know that we are all headed somewhere, but most people do not call life a journey. They simply call it "living." The word "journey" is found sixty times in the Bible and every time it denoted movement.

Dedicated To:

In our lives there are many people whom we interact with. People who affect our lives, either positively or negatively. On the journey through life, the Lord Jesus positions people in the place where they can have a real Godly effect on the lives of others. I know that if it had not been for these listed, I cannot say what my journey would have been like. I thank the Lord continually for the spiritual effect they had on my journey through life, helping me to fulfill God's call and purpose for my life.

Bernice Clark
My Mother (In Heaven)

Rev. Willard (JJ) Johnson
My Husband (In Heaven)

Rev. Charles H Harrell
First Pastor & mentor

Rev. Ken Cloudus
Community Christian Center
(Ordaining & mentoring)

Journey's Definition

Webster's Definition: The act or instance of traveling from one place to another; Any course or passage from one stage or experience to another.

Vine's Definition: To travel, to be on the way, taking a trip from one place to another, to move or set forward; Sojourning from one place to another; to go forward.

Young's definition: to go away, to pass from one place to another, to send forward, to lift up, to pass throughout, to pass on or forward.

Life itself is a journey. When we are born into this world, we begin the journey through life. It begins with infancy and how long and where the journey takes you and how you get there depends on several things. Eph. 4:17 tells us, that, *"We are born in iniquity, shaped in sin, walking the way of the world."* This is how we all begin the journey of life. Since the fall of man in the Garden of Eden when Adam and Eve disobeyed God and ate from the tree they were told not to, the journey God planned for them was diverted. God was no longer the navigator of the journey they would take. The first, or the beginning, of the journey they would take would now take them from the garden and the presence of God.

Every person born on earth after the fall would be born in sin and begin the journey of destruction and finally hell. Matt. 7:13. (KJV) *"Wide is the gate and broad is the way that leadeth to destruction, and many there be which go in there at."*

Every person born on the earth is free to make the choice as to which path or way they will take on the journey of life. It makes it easier in the natural to choose the path for your journey through life. But God, who is not willing that any should perish, had a plan before the earth was created to create another path. That path was established when Jesus came to the earth as a man born of a virgin, the way no one had been born without the seed of a man. *God who is not willing that any should perish,* sent Jesus, the third person of the God Head Body to rescue us from the path of destruction, to rescue us from the journey to hell.

God told Jeremiah that before he was formed in his mother's womb, He knew him and predestined a specific path (journey) to take. Jer. 29:11(NLT) *for I know the plans I have for you.* God has a plan for our lives. The plan begins with accepting Jesus as Lord and savior, giving Him the right to reveal to us the path for the journey we are saved from hell to complete. On this journey, there will be many different experiences.... Matt 7:14, *"Straight is the gate, and narrow is the way, which leadeth unto life and few there be that find it."* Not all the experiences on the journey that God planned for us will be pleasant, but He said that He would be with us and would not forsake us. If on the journey it seems if we are walking alone, can we say that we are walking the path that God has set for us? Psalms 16:11, "Thou wilt show me the path of life: in thy presence there is fullness of joy; at thy right hand there are pleasures for evermore."

Not all the experiences on the journey that God planned for us will be pleasant. We cannot use the joy or sorrow that we experience on the journey of life as a determining factor as to whether we are where God preordained us to be. Remember, on this journey we are in the enemy's territory. and the Lord said that He would be with us. If on the journey it seems as if you are walking alone, can you say that you are walking the path that God set you on? Remember that Satan claims to be the traffic director in the earth. We see in the scriptures where many of God's servants got off the path of the journey that God predestined for their lives. Saul, Samson, David, Judas, Peter and others got off the path they were set to walk on. Some got back on the predestined path and finished their journey, fulfilling the call of God on their lives. Some never got back to the path of their predestined journey.

This is not a story of perfection, but a thankful acknowledgement to almighty God for the journey HE set before me, and His faithfulness in directing, correcting and protecting me throughout the journey. God carried me through times of difficulty when I didn't know which path to take. I could not have even imagined me being able to travel the path that He set before me, a path that I shunned for many years. But thanks be unto God who always causes us to triumph in Him!

I was, as we all were, born in sin as the word tells us. On a path that I walked for many years, walking in worldly success, thinking that this was God blessing me, even though I didn't know Him. But there comes a time when we have the opportunity to change paths, to get off the path or journey that leads to destruction and begin to walk a new way. The Lord told Joshua and the children of Israel in Joshua 24:15, *"Choose you this day whom you will serve."* There comes a time when we must make a decision as to which path we're going to walk. When we accept the Lord as our Savior, the direction for our journey is changed because our destination has changed. The path of our journey changes. We are no longer on the path to hell, where we were walking in darkness, but in Christ we are walking a path that is illuminated. Prov. 4:18, *"The path of the just is as a shining light."* And just as we are given a DMV manual to study before we take the test in order to begin to drive a vehicle, God has given us a manual to study in order for us to be able to navigate His vehicle to the destination that He has preordained for each of us. IT IS THE BIBLE—His words of instruction.

When we're born into the world, we begin a journey that is directed into hell. Because of the sin of Adam and Eve, everyone born on earth is born in sin. That is why Jesus came, in order that we would have an option—a choice of two paths to choose from. In Joshua 24:15, God tells His people to, *"Choose you this day whom ye will serve."* There is a continual drawing by the Spirit of God to take us off the path that we walk from our birth. God is an awesome God; He continually tries to draw us from the path that we walk from our birth. The choice is ours. There are many people in hell today who chose to continue on the path that was leading them there. God gives us a choice. He will not force us to serve Him.

When my life began, until I became old enough to make a choice of the path I would walk, I was in a place of God's protection from hell. I was born in a family of seven children in Dekalb, Mississippi. This was during a time of great difficulty for black families in the south. My parents were farmers. It was a very hard time in a very small farming town. It seems as if Satan knows when God's hand is upon newly born children He has chosen for His purpose. The early experiences of my life were not pleasant. To begin with, both of my grandmothers were the product of rape by their mother's slave owners. My grandfather on my father's side was lynched while the family was at church on a Sunday morning. The report was that he killed himself. But he could not have hung himself from such a high branch without his horse which was used to pull the wagon with the family to church.

Satan used many racial episodes to bring fear and submission to those close to me. I experienced my relatives hiding men in the forest so they could get them safely out of Mississippi to prevent their lynching. I know now that Satan's plan was to build hatred and fear in my life, as the memories of these events never left me. It created fear, but not hatred, for God had other plans for my life and hatred would cause me to walk another path that God didn't plan for me. We attended a Mississippi Baptist church. During that time there was very little of God's word taught. The idea was, if you attended church on Sunday, you were alright with God, and would go to heaven, regardless to how you were living. The sinner's prayer was not a part of the church, just a handshake with the pastor.

When I was seven years old, in the third grade, we moved to Phoenix, Arizona. It was more than seventy-five years later that I was told that the reason for the move was to protect my mother from being raped by a very prosperous Caucasian man who had great authority in Dekalb. He hired many of the black men to work for him, including my father. My mother would clean their house sometime. She was a very beautiful, shy woman who did not interact with men outside of our family. This move had no advance planning. We were packed up swiftly and taken to my grandmother's house in Meridian, Mississippi withing two days without us kids knowing in advance about the move. After the move, my dad left several days later to go to Phoenix, leaving the farm that he owned before he and my mother were married. He just abandoned it. All of this had a lifelong effect on my father and his attitude.

We as kids adjusted to the move as we had no choice. It seemed as if light was shining a little brighter to illuminate the path of life for us as kids. Three months later we took a train to join my father in Phoenix. This was in 1942, and World War II was just beginning. For us, this was a time of changing values and spiritual environment. Phoenix was a city with three military bases nearby. So, there was much variety in the lives of people living there. The churches did not have the same impact and influence that it had in the country environment.

We lived on a farm outside of Phoenix but could not attend the local schools because of the segregated school laws. So, every school day we were awakened at five o'clock in the morning, walked two miles to the city bus stop, rode to downtown Phoenix where we took another bus that took us to the school (Dunbar) that we attended. We were raised under very strict parenting, as my father, Horace who worked for the Phoenix School district demanded that we excelled in every area of education because all of the teachers knew him and kept him advised of what was going on in our school lives. During summer when other children played all day, we were given schoolwork to do, and he would grade it. He was very strict. He demanded that we represent the family well.

My father became a weekend alcoholic. He was very jealous and abusive to my mother who was a beautiful woman and demanded that she not have friends outside of family contacts. This was very difficult for us as children. He chose our friends and as girls we were to have no boys as friends. When I was in the eighth grade, he and his best friend had a weekly Saturday night drinking binge from bar to bar. One Saturday, as they moved from one bar to another, the convertible his friend was driving while intoxicated, when he was parking, drove under a flatbed truck on the passenger side, and my father suffered severe injuries. He was transported to the hospital where he was scheduled for surgery in the morning.

My mother was taken to the hospital when the word came about the accident. She was sent home planning to return before the surgery began. He passed away before she arrived at the hospital. This was a very difficult time for my family, as my mother had married my father at sixteen years old, and never worked outside of the home. My older sister, Pauline had just married and my older brother, Horace (HP) was a freshman at Carver High School, and I was ready to graduate from the eighth grade to go to high school. This was a new direction for my family. My gentle, loving mother was now the head of a family of six children, ages ranging from one and a half years to fifteen years old.

After my father's funeral, we moved into a different house. We did not want to continue to live where there were so many memories. This was the beginning of a new journey. Not for me, but for my mother and my sister, Dallas, and my brother Tally. I know now that the house we moved into was the plan of God. On the next street was a Pentecostal church. Several of my sister's friends were members of that church of God in Christ, so my sister, Dallas began to attend along with my brother Tally. Within several weeks, they received the Lord and went through the process that the church called "tarrying" for the Holy Ghost. They were filled after a period. By then, my mother had begun to attend the church with them. After several weeks of attending day and night meetings, one night she was brought home by a group of people carrying her. When they knocked on the door and I opened it, it was terrifying to see my mother seemingly dead. After losing my father, I was so afraid. As they laid her on the sofa, one of the men and his wife said to me, she's alright and then they left. They did not tell me what had happened to her. I can't explain the fear that had gripped me. From time to time she would speak what I called gibberish. Now I know she was speaking in tongues as she had been filled with the Holy Spirit. My mother and my sister and brother's life changed. The impact on my life was major.

My brother in high school, Horace, whom we called HP, did not seem to be concerned about the change as he now had the freedom to be active with his High School activities. I felt abandoned as the only thing that had not changed was my young sister Fredna, who was four years old and my brother Darrell who was two. I was an honor student getting ready to graduate from grammar school when it was told to my class that one High School in Phoenix was being desegregated and some graduating students from our school, Mary Bethune School would be permitted to attend Phoenix Technical High School if they desired. The ones to attend were chosen. I had been feeling so detached from everything because of all the changes in those who were closest to me, it didn't matter where I went. I was among the students chosen to be part of the desegregating group of students.

Coming from a neighborhood that had only Blacks, Mexicans, and Indians, who could only attend Black, Mexican or Indian schools, this was very hard to adjust to as it was like Mississippi. The only thing was, I was now old enough for the treatment to be more damaging because I could understand what was happening. The staff at the school basically ignored us. For two years, all the students integrating the school could not get a grade higher than a C. I can say that it could have had a very negative impact on my life, but my mother's prayers and the expectation that my father had for our educational future did not diminish in my heart. The third year there, things began to change. Some of the black male students became great football and basketball players who helped the school to excel in sports that they had never experienced. It was the catapult into the office profession for me and other students who had no opportunity before. I participated in school activities and began to go to dances and parties outside of school. My life was headed in a direction that was totally contrary to my mother's desire for me. I realize now that Satan used my fear of Pentecostalism to take me in a direction away from the Lord. I ran from any real contact with the Lord or Christianity. This was Satan's plan to assure that I would never get on the path of my journey with the Lord.

My teenage life was worldly. My mother's prayers kept me from many paths that were often before me. I know now that the strict teachings of my dad had something to do with it too. Also, many of my friend's parents were church members too. They were not pentecostalist but committed to their denominations. In my last year in high school, I began seriously dating the man that I would marry, Willard Johnson. He was such a gentle, loving, and respectful person. Very different from his friends whom he served with in the Air Force. He was stationed at Williams Air Force Base in Chandler, Arizona which was thirty miles from Phoenix. So, he would be with me on weekends for parties, dances at Riverside Ballroom where famous bands and groups would come to perform, picnics and USO gatherings with military members.

During all this time I was so busy with school and my social life I did not know what was happening with my mother, Bernice Clark. She had begun to attend meetings held by Reverend A.A. Allen, a worldwide evangelist and prophet, whose ministry was based in Phoenix. He held tent meetings at a local park near our house. Her pastor did not sanction her attending, as a word was being taught about the power of God and faith in God that at that time few if any churches taught. She would come home from the meetings with so many tales of miracles and manifestations of the Spirit of God with people being delivered from demons. She would tell of the demons leaving one person and going into another person. She would tell of people's eyes being healed from blindness, legs growing, growths leaving people's bodies. I did not know how to take this because I never knew my mother to tell a lie. I once went by the park where the meetings were being held. There were so many people there, the biggest tent I had ever seen could not hold them. There was a fence of people surrounding the tent. I never went back. But I later learned that many of the great faith and healing ministers were basically birthed in these meetings. My mother became a part of the staff, was an intercessor, ordained an evangelist and catapulted into the world to minister to the lost. She preached on skid row in Phoenix, Los Angeles and three countries. I was amazed at this quiet, humble woman's boldness and spiritual power.

The path that I was on was not as horrible as it could have been if not for the prayers of my mother and her sisters in the Lord. I knew nothing about this. When my last year in high school ended, I had just turned seventeen in March. My sweetheart Willard, who his military buddies nicknamed Grapenuts, because he ate lots of that cereal and who was also called JJ short for Junior Johnson because he was named after his father, asked me to marry him. My mother gave her permission, as did his commanding officer at the base. My mother loved JJ because she saw his character was not a wild one. Also, I know she felt that this would get me off the path that she didn't know where it would lead me to. I'm sure she knew that the journey I was on was leading me to hell as she frequently told me. I was not drinking and doing drugs, just partying, playing cards and being part of the drill team and dances, which was definitely not godly in her mind. There was a park in the black community called East Lake Park that held a weekly teenage dance on Sunday night with chaperones. So, while they were in church, I was attending the dance.

My mother and my friend Helen Cochran accompanied us to the chapel as I had to have permission because at that time anyone who married before their 21st birthday had to have parental and military permission. My aunt Ruth gave us a wedding reception. After our marriage, I found out that JJ was as innocent as I was, but because he was a Staff Sargent, he pretended to be like the other guys. Which is what I thought also. God altered the path that we both would walk. He had a plan that He was not ready for us to fulfill because we were not ready. We only went to church for funerals and weddings, as JJ only had a casual Methodist church experience. JJ's military service was during the Korean War. Three of his close friends lost their lives in the war. But he was not deployed to the battlefield. I know now that it was the prayers of the saints that kept him home because all his unit eventually was deployed. We lived in an apartment in a housing project, built in South Phoenix from where JJ commuted thirty-six miles daily to get to the base. Our daughter Linda was born the next year when he only had six months before his enlistment term was over. They tried to get him to reenlist, but had we agreed that he would not reenlist.

After his discharge, we moved to his hometown of Wichita, Kansas. He and I both went back to school. He as a tool and die maker and I to become a nurse. After he finished, he went to work at Boeing Aircraft, installing engines in new planes. And I became pregnant again with our second child, Jacquelyn. She was born with serious medical conditions resulting from a birth defect. After several near-death experiences, the doctor suggested that we should move from the cold climate. So, our journey brought us to California. During all this time there was no contact with God, except my mother and the saints in Phoenix praying for us. After we relocated to Los Angeles, we made contact with a cousin whose husband was the pastor of a Baptist church. We began to attend Sunday services and I sang in the choir. But I knew nothing about accepting the Lord and the sinner's prayer.

My husband JJ was a Federal Postal employee in Los Angeles and after we were in Los Angeles two years, we bought a home in Compton, California. After we were there two years our son Tracy was born. I had begun to attend a Baptist church but was not faithful because I still was not a believer. So, when the opportunity came for my young children to attend the Catholic school nearby, we enrolled them there and took classes to learn about Catholicism. Without knowing the word of God, the Priests teachings seemed to be exciting and the real explanation of all that took place in the plan of God for salvation. So, my whole family became Catholics. We thought this was salvation. There was no confession to the Lord for our sins, nor asking Him to receive us as His children. But we were faithful to the teachings of Catholicism. I worked with the Nuns and in the school. During this time, I was also working in my nursing career in several hospitals.

After five years, the atmosphere in our Southern California community had changed. There was much violence and riots taking place. So, we bought a home in Valinda/La Puente, California. My children moved to the catholic schools in West Covina. We were still very faithful to our Catholic faith. Within six months after our relocation, after having a physical exam, I was called by my doctor's office to come in because my pap smear came back showing cancer. I had been having some female problems, but I was so busy being a wife and mother, I didn't give it much thought. But when I went in for a more extended physical, the results came back showing cervical and ovarian cancer.

Being in the medical profession, this was a traumatic situation. My thought was where is this going to take us? My doctor was in Lynwood, California, so surgery was planned immediately. Being so far from a relationship with the Lord, all I could do was what Catholics do, pray their prayers, going through Mary and Saints. The surgery was performed, and I seemed to have a good recovery. This was before chemotherapy, but they did give me radium implants. After recovery, I was getting back to being a wife and mother. Within six months, I began to have pain that was worse than before I had the surgery. Going back to the doctor, I was told that the cancer had spread. This was devastating to me. I knew the result of cancer's spreading after having surgery. I became depressed, began to take medicine to fight the stress. As the pain increased, I had no choice but to go back for another surgery. My mother was praying for me, but I still did not believe that I needed to be like my Pentecostal family. I believed that what I was doing was what God wanted me to do.

So, going back to the hospital for another surgery, it never occurred to me that I might not make it through this time. It never occurred to me that if I didn't make it, I would go to hell. After all, according to the teaching of the church I was a member of, there is always purgatory where I would stay for a while and then go on to heaven. Sometimes we don't know how far we have advanced in the journey that we are on, and even though I didn't, my mother did. I wanted nothing to do with the Pentecostal religion. My mother never laid hands on me because she knew that I did not want her to. The thing that did take place I had no say about. My mother's brother, uncle

Sam, who was a deacon in a Spirit filled Church in Phoenix, flew in one day to pray for me. He was such an authoritative Christian that I certainly did not tell him no.

Even though I did not want anyone to pray for me in the hospital before my surgery, my mother had intercessors in the waiting room, and I understand that they were praying there. I think about it now and I wonder how that went about since praying in tongues for them was not quiet. All I know is she would not give up on me. I believe she knew the plan that God had for my life. During the surgery, my heart stopped but they brought me back. I was brought out of the anesthesia and was told that I would have an injection that would make me numb from my waist down so they could continue the surgery. I went back to sleep and awaken in my room the next day and was told that they had to remove some of my intestines. My recovery was slow, pain and depression were constant. We had a very large swimming pool, and I didn't know how to swim, and one day I found myself standing by the deep end of the pool. I was home alone and I was planning to jump in the pool and kill myself to keep JJ and the kids from going through what I knew was ahead of me. My mother was praying for me at her house, and the thought came to me (I know now that it was God responding to mother's prayer) that they would suffer more if they had to deal with my suicide, and that if I had more time with them to prepare them for my departure it would be easier on them. I walked away from the pool.

I was prepared to die, but God had other plans. Thank God for the saints that continued to intercede for my salvation. I didn't die. I gradually got stronger and came out of the depressed state I was in. The pain gradually left. There were some aftereffects, but they were not debilitating. I chose not to go back to the doctors again. And after about a year and a half, I received a letter from my doctor to find out if I was still alive. I never responded. I was alive and able to resume my life as it was. We were still active in the catholic church.

As time passed, my girls were attending Bishop Amat Catholic High School in West Covina when the Jesus Movement was in full blast. Many of their catholic friends were accepting the Lord and being filled with the Holy Spirit. When the girls finished high school, they went to Mt Sac College in the city of Walnut. Linda was engaged to a Vietnam veteran who was also attending. One Sunday night she, Jackie and a cousin went to a church in Los Angeles, which was a Church of God in Christ. The same Pentecostal denomination that my mother, sister, and brother belonged to. They came home and stayed in the car for a long period of time. Since I knew they were there, I went out to see why they were still in the car. As I went toward the car, I heard them speaking in tongues. I knew that they were now following the path of my mother, sister, and brother. But I did not have fear because of the environment that they were exposed to, I knew that this may be a protection to keep them from falling prey to it.

By this time, I had gone back to college because I no longer wanted to be in the medical profession. I chose to major in agronomy since JJ and I had purchased land in Alamosa, Colorado, with plans to move there when Tracy graduated from high school. It is amazing how Satan lays before you an easy path to what seems like a real great future for you, when it is only a way to take you farther away from the path that God has for you to walk. When Tracy graduated from high school, his plan was to remain in the area, so he attended Mt Sac college also. So, our plan for Colorado was abandoned. Which meant that since we were not going to be farmers, I had to add another major to my college career. I chose communications. By now all my children were grown. And JJ and I began to fall away from the Catholic Church. One day one of my classmates shared Jesus with me in a manner that I now know was scriptural and it made sense to me. She asked me if I wanted to accept Jesus as my Lord. I said to her, "Not now, when I finish school and have my career secure, I will do it."

My daughters found a church in Walnut, California. The church was a newly formed Spirit filled ministry pastored by Rev. Charles Harrell. Linda had met him as she commuted back and forth to her job in Los Angeles by bus. Every day, she found herself on the bus driven by Pastor Charles, who worked for the L.A. Transit Department. He ministered the word to the people who took the last of the trip each day, being only a few at the end of the line. He invited them to his home where the church was meeting. On Sunday they met in an auditorium at Mt. Sac college. They were excited about the church. They became faithful attendees.

The church, at the girl's request began to pray for their father and my salvation. By that time, we were only attending the Catholic church on "Holy Days" only. I began to get an urge to visit a local Baptist church that a neighbor attended. At least, I thought, they are not as radical as Holy Ghost filled churches, and maybe everyone will be satisfied. The Southern Baptist church was located in La Puente, where I began attending and soon joined. I said "joined." I became a member of the church, not a member of the family of God. No one led me in the sinner's prayer of which I knew nothing about. I attended regularly, weekly Bible study and Sunday service and grew very little in the knowledge of God as the Word of God was not alive unto me. By this time, I had graduated from college and was working as a Public Relations Specialist for a major company and writing for their monthly news booklet. I was also free lancing as a journalist and public relations specialist.

By this time, I was at the point of leaving the church completely, for I saw little difference between who I was and most of the people in this church. I was looking for a change, I was ready for it. I had begun to watch Christian TV. I watched Jimmy Swaggart, Fred Price, Kenneth Hagan, Lester Sumrall, and others who taught the word of God plainly and it made a difference in my life. I prayed the sinner's prayer through Christian TV, asking the Lord to come into my heart and help me to live for Him. But I continued to attend the Baptist Church. The atmosphere did not change, and there was a seemingly empty place inside of me. By now JJ had begun to attend church with me. He "joined" the church also. No sinner's prayer, just a handshake. One day, it was announced on TBN, the Christian broadcast station, that Jimmy Swaggart was going to be coming to the Long Beach Conference Center for a three-day Convention. My brother asked me if I wanted to go to the Friday session from work as we both worked in downtown Los Angeles. I agreed to go. He picked me up after work and I had a glimpse of what serving God was really like. The word was preached, truth without watering it down. Afterwards, I saw real spiritual ministry, healing, deliverance, and Holy Spirit infilling. I had never been in an environment that seemed to have tangible aspects. I hungered for more.

Where did this hunger come from? How can we begin the journey without someone praying? My daughter Jackie had begun to pray with a group of women from her church, Walnut Faith Center who was now holding Sunday service in the auditorium at Mt. San Antonio College in Walnut, California. JJ and I were one of the targets. I was being reeled in. My mother, sister, Dallas and brother, Tally invited JJ and I to go back to the Sunday evening service of Jimmy Swaggart. The Convention center was pack to the rafters. We had to sit in the very top seats in the arena. The service was so anointed. I recognize it now, but then I didn't really know what was taking place. I now know that the presence of the Lord had invaded the place.

After the message, he gave the altar call, Then, he called for anyone wishing to receive the Holy Spirit. I hadn't even thought about it. But I jumped up immediately and began the journey down the steps to the front. JJ thought we were going down for refreshments, so he followed me. He had no idea why I turned towards the front. Jimmy Swaggart led us in a prayer of salvation and the prayer for receiving the Holy Spirit, asking the Holy Spirit to fall on those of us standing before him.

I don't know what they felt on the day of Pentecost when the Holy Spirit fell on the 120 in the upper room, but I can tell you what happened to me. I felt as if I was being electrocuted, but not painfully so. But filled with so much power, I couldn't move. I was paralyzed with my arms lifted up to God. I began to speak in a language, not stammering or murmuring, but a language. I knew that I was not just speaking in tongues, but I was prophesying and proclaiming. Was I proclaiming God's plan and will for my future? I was speaking in a voice that reverberated throughout the whole arena. It certainly was not my flesh. I knew nothing about what was taking place, nor did I care. My husband, JJ stood beside me embarrassed, for he knew less than I did. Truly, I was beginning a journey that I could not navigate by myself. I could not move—the only part of me that had any motion was my mouth and tongue.

I don't know how long I was frozen in that position. I was aware of people leaving the arena. The service was over. I was aware of people walking past me with smiles on their faces. Perhaps they knew what was happening to me, but I truly did not. I'm sure that JJ was not understanding what was happening to his sophisticated, proper wife. When finally, I began to be able to have mobility, I was still in another place. We walked to the car. He didn't know what to say, I didn't know how to explain to him what was going on. Every time I would begin to speak, I ended up speaking in tongues. Now I understood what had happened to my mother when they brought her home after she was filled with the Holy Spirit, when I was so frightened. Only now I was not frightened, just amazed.

When we arrived home, I was still in the Spirit. I needed to be alone to see if I could figure out what was going on. I didn't think the tradition in my mother would be able to address what was happening to me. I was wrong I found out later, as she had had a similar experience, though not as radical. I shut myself away and couldn't shut God out. Nor could I shut the words up that were pouring from me. I know now that I could have just refused to utter—but I needed to know what God was doing and where He was taking me with this new life. The next day I awakened a new person. I looked the same, but inside I was not. It was if I had had a renewal inwardly. I was so excited. I couldn't wait to tell the people at my (Baptist) church. At the Tuesday night Bible study, I announced that I had been baptized in the Holy Ghost and spoke in tongues. You could have heard a pin hit the floor. I had no idea it would be taken in that manner. Afterwards, I asked the pastor if I could speak with him. Explaining what had happened to me. I thought he could give me some insight scripturally as to what had happened to me. His response was not a good one, causing me to doubt if what happened was God.

But it was too late. I was convinced that God was in control of my life. So, I picked up my Bible and began a journey that changed me forever. The journey, like the baptism of the Holy Spirit was a supernatural one, I walked with Jesus through the four entire gospels. It was a supernatural experience. Each day as I rode the bus to my place of employment, I was walking with Jesus, seeing and hearing what the scriptures were depicting. In the evening, I would be so far from the natural realm, I frequently went miles pass my bus stop, having to ride to the end of the line and then back to where I should have gotten off in the beginning. I saw and understood Jesus's journey and the words He spoke. Each day I resumed my journey with Jesus, getting to know the Lord whom I had rejected for so many years.

Even at that time I did not know that not every believer had the experience that I was having. I couldn't explain it to anyone. Since my pastor was now rejecting me as if I was a contagious person with a life taking disease. Persecution began, but I didn't pick up on it because I was so swept off into the realm of the supernatural. By this time JJ had come to the church to become a member. No salvation offered, just a handshake by the pastor and deacon. Afterwards, they held a brotherly cigarette smoke on the outside the church as they welcomed him into the church. Not into the kingdom of God. As time went on, we were faithful attenders of the church. But I was not treated as a faithful member. One incident took place that brought things to the place where even JJ could not ignore what was going on.

The church was invited to go to another church

to a meeting on a Sunday night. Our pastor was to be the speaker and the choir, which I was a part of, sang. Something happened that was similar to my experience when I was filled with the Holy Spirit. As the choir was sitting down after singing, I couldn't sit down. I was frozen in a standing position with that electricity flowing through my body. As it flowed up to my mouth, I began to speak in tongues. At that time, I did not know that I was prophesying, even though the words were flowing in my head. I did not know that all I had to do was to begin speaking those words and that God wanted to exhort the people. Nor did I know that this was supposedly a Spirit filled Baptist church.

When finally, the Presence of the Lord eased off me, and I was able to sit, I felt the rejection of all those I had embraced as my church family. Everyone's eyes stayed on me. It was a very discomforting situation, but I must say, it was only the beginning of many on this journey with the Lord. I was just beginning to experience the rejection that Jesus received because of the path He chose to walk. If I had not had the supernatural experience of walking with Jesus on His journey I don't know if I could have gone on. I had ridden to the church with the pastor, his wife and two of the sisters in the church. Needless to say, it was a very uncomfortable ride back home. Nothing was said, but the silence spoke much. No one talked but to say good night to me when I got out of the car. I kept asking the Lord what happened, what did I do wrong? How was I supposed to handle what happened?

One thing I learned from this experience was that I needed to be taught about what was going on in my life, and I was not being taught where I was. But if I just left, what would happen to JJ? For he had become comfortable in the church. If I just left, I was concerned that he would stop going at all. The situation did not improve, in fact it got to the place where JJ realized what was going on. Since he knew, I prayed for the Lord to show me what to do. I suggested that we go to church with the girls on their Bible study night, which was now being held in a member's home, and to their Sunday night service. As we did begin to attend, JJ was comfortable there, as Pastor Charles was very friendly and spiritually led by the Lord. We still attended the church we had joined, but it was not the same as we begin to experience the presence of the Lord at Walnut Faith Center. When I sat down at this church on the first Sunday night visit, I knew that I was being led by the Lord. The word of God was taught that begin to take me beyond my Pentecostal experience. Teaching on how God speaks today, being led by the Spirit of the Lord, the purpose of the Holy Spirit, how to walk in the Spirit and not the flesh, forgiveness, humility, God's purpose and plans for each of us. It was as if heaven opened up and I was sitting at the feet of Jesus.

The second Sunday night, I went up for prayer, to know the will of God for my life. I was enrolled in the master's program at Fullerton State College, planning to be a college professor. As Pastor Charles laid hands on me, he began to speak of God's plan for me, to be a teacher, to make a difference in the lives of many people. I came away rejoicing because I felt it confirmed what I had planned for my life. Little did I know how wrong I was. JJ and I decided that we wanted to be a part of Walnut Faith Center, so we invited our pastor to our home to inform him that we would be leaving the church. As we explained that we felt that we did not fit in at the church because of the difference of biblical interpretation. He let JJ know that it is because of me that this was happening. We embraced him as he left and pronounced blessings on his ministry and the church. I thought we had handled it in a godly manner. The next week I saw him at the Post Office, and he turned away from me without speaking. *("For as many as are led by the Spirit of the Lord, they are the sons of God."* Rom. 8:14)

This turn in the journey was an exciting experience. An adventure never experienced before. Jer. 1:5, *"Before I formed thee in the belly, I knew thee; and before thou camest forth out of the womb I sanctified thee, and I ordained thee a prophet unto the nations."* We totally submitted ourselves to the Lord and the church, to do whatever we could. Remember, JJ had not yet accepted the Lord, thinking that going to church and doing the work was being saved. That soon changed as we were faithful Bible study attendees. During the Bible studies, as we praised the Lord, the presence of the Lord was present in the home where we met. Many times, I experienced the anointing that basically paralyzed me as it had at the church that night. I know that at first, Pastor Charles didn't realize that it was the power of God that immobilized me. But he soon realized that God's hand was upon me. It was somewhat difficult to adjust to this, as it made me seem like a weird woman.

One thing that I appreciated about Pastor Charles was that he did not quickly place people in a position. He had to get to know you, spiritually and naturally, consequently, he had truly dedicated, anointed people working in the church. No favoritism or position because of who you were or what you knew. As for me, I knew nothing and could not and would not play the Christianese game. This part of my journey became one where I had to be still and see the salvation of the Lord. I shut myself away because I did not speak Christianese and could not fake it. I did not know that I was moving into the place where God intended to perfect that which He had placed in me in my mother's womb. He began to bring it to life when I had that experience at the Jimmy Swaggart conference. I felt that I couldn't pray like everyone else, I couldn't speak, and act like them. So, when I shut myself away, I didn't stop doing what I was doing, but I spent hours every day on my face before the Lord. I would pray with my understanding, but it was mostly, "I'm sorry Lord that I can't do anything for you." I can only say that God took charge of that time and as I began to talk to God about my inability, He began to take me into the Spirit, no more talking in the natural. He controlled the situation and I let Him.

I had many supernatural experiences during this time, some of which I will tell as we move along. But during this time, which was around two years, He took me on the spiritual journey of my life. If I had known that this was what would be happening in my life I would have perhaps run from God. I didn't know that the multitudes of people in the congregation beneath the speaker's platform that I saw while I was praying were listening to me ministering. I didn't know that the oceans that I saw were the oceans I would be flying over and that the tunnel of darkness that a beacon of light shining from an individual, leading multitudes from the darkness was me, as I was interceding for souls. I didn't know the giant serpent that was stretched before me was my confrontations with Satan. I didn't really know what was happening as I prayed, and the Lord was giving me these visions. Then one day I was praying and in the spirit, I saw a plane making a landing at an airport, the plane veered off the landing path and headed toward the airport building. The intensity of my prayer increased, and I saw the plane stop before it reached the building. I made nothing of it as I was having many of this kind of visions without knowing what was happening. But that evening on the news, I saw exactly what I had seen in the vision. All the lives were saved. I am sure that others were praying for that situation also.

As I grew in the plan of God for my life, I began to be active in the ministry at the church, the plan to be a college professor faded away. I was totally sold out to the plan of God for my life. Truly having no knowledge or desire for where He was taking me. I began to be active in the ministry at Walnut Faith Center, working with the women's fellowship and attending the Word of Faith Bible Training Center. I taught a weekly bible study during the day. I realized that perhaps God never intended for me to be a secular teacher. In fact, He brought me out of secular employment with power and wrath. Heb. 10:31, AMP, *"It is a fearful (formidable and terrible) thing to incur the divine penalties and be cast into the hands of the living God!"*

Before I had shut myself away to be with the Lord, I had several encounters with Him that I must admit I was not pleased with what He was saying to me. One was the first time I heard Him speak to me in that quiet voice that penetrated my spirit. I had a problem that was costing us financially, brought on by someone else. After all the teaching I had on trusting God and walking by faith, it seemed that God wasn't moving fast enough. I came home from work very troubled. I went into my bedroom and cried out to God, "Lord, I didn't have this kind of problem when I was in the world!" The voice of the Lord came to me, not to my ears, but inside of me I heard his voice saying, "Go to the window." I didn't know what to expect to see, perhaps the answer to this financial problem. I stood looking out of the window. I saw nothing that was not there before. As I was beginning to express my disappointment, the words came to me (not naturally, but my spiritual ears were opened) "Be still and listen." It seemed as if my ears popped open and I heard what sounded like thousands of birds in the tree before me chirping and singing. Before I could speak, the Lord quoted a scripture that I had just covered a few days earlier. Matt. 6:26, *"Behold the fowls of the air: for they sow not, neither do they reap, nor gather into barns; yet your heavenly Father feedeth them. Are ye not much better than they?"*

I took this as God's promise to look after me. The second encounter in which the Lord let me see another side of Him was concerning the position that I held with a major company after I finished my degree in communication, journalism, and public relation. In the world we would say this is a job I'd kill for. And the

Lord spoke to my spirit and told me to come away from my job. I tried to ignore the voice. Remember, *the Spirit of the Lord will not always strive with man.* You may wonder why, besides pride, that I didn't want to leave my position. JJ had been a manager for a chain drug store for twelve years, and during my last year in college he left the position to go in business with his brother Bob. When we came to the Lord, the business changed, and his brother closed it down. His financial position was different than ours, so why would God call me away from my job at this time? I said, "No Way!"

The prompting of the Lord was less and less as time went on. One morning I came into my office, opened a drawer to put my purse into it, and just as my spiritual ears opened to hear the birds—my nostrils popped open, and an odor penetrated my nostrils that was so repugnant that I almost vomited. The crazy thing is, I knew immediately what it was. I was smelling the stench I was sending up to God because of my rebellion. Luke 14:33, *"So likewise, whosoever he be of you that forsaketh not all that he hath, he cannot be my disciple."* I didn't need the Lord to tell me, I knew. It was so frightening, I grabbed my purse and ran to the restroom and shut myself in a stall, shaking with fear. I made it through the day, but when I got home, I said to JJ, "The Lord said I have to quit my job." I thought he would be upset and question the validity of what I was saying. All he said was, "If the

Lord said to do it, you have to do it." What a wonderful man the Lord blessed me with. He didn't say, "How are we going to make it?" or "What are we going to do?" Remember, he had not yet said the sinner's prayer. But was a faithful church attender. He helped to make my journey so much easier.

The next week I gave two weeks' notice. I didn't know where this would all end, but the faith teaching I was receiving at our church was strengthening me for the journey. During the two weeks before my last day on the job, JJ had applied at the federal building for the job he had held for many years before he went with the Drug Store as a manager. It is amazing how God worked things out. They rehired him, the twelve years he was away was applied to his employee status and the week after I left my job, he was working full time for the federal government. Even after all my experience of disobeying the Lord, temptation came, and I succumbed to it. A classmate of mine called me about an opportunity to do a public relations job for the National MBA Association of America's annual conference which would be held in Los Angeles. They were seeking someone to do the advertising and publicity. I had the contacts, so I agreed to work with my friend (who was not a Christian) to do the publicity for the event. The money I would get was needed. I had TV, Radio, and Newspaper connections. So, I figured that it would be easy to get it done.

I did not consider that I was moving in disobedience to the Lord who had called me away from secular work. Gen 6:3, *"My spirit shall not always strive with man, for that he also is flesh."* You must understand that this kind of national meeting of professional people was not just an innocent kind of gathering. There were all sorts of sinful activities needed to be planned for. (Women, drugs, alcohol and whatever else was demanded.) I took no part in any of these demands and suffered the consequences financially. The event was to be held at a major hotel in downtown Los Angeles. All of a sudden, all of my contacts were not available. It seemed as if I would fail in the public relations job of publicity for the conference. When I prayed and asked the Lord to open those shut doors, the Spirit of the Lord revealed to me that I was in disobedience to the Lord. I was not trusting Him to provide for my needs, so I did what He had called me away from. I wept and repented, crying out to the Lord to forgive me. I saw myself as a rebellious person and I was willing to fail in what He had called me away from. The next day all the shut doors began to open. God is so good to us, even when we have not trusted Him. The event was a success. But I knew that I would never do that again. All God wants from us is to be willing and obedient. Isa. 1:19, *"If ye be willing and obedient, ye shall eat the good of the land."*

I began to see what God was doing. Not only did I

see it, but I understood why He was stripping from me all that I put before Him, everything that had my affection in a way that was worldly. One night, after returning from Bible study, as I was undressing and hanging my clothes in the closet, the Lord spoke to my spirit to remove the clothes from the closet and give them away. I was a stylist, clothes and jewelry and perfume was what I collected, not just stuff, but expensive stuff. So, I began to lay out what was not special or valuable to me. As I thought that I had done what God was leading me to do, I gathered the few garments together and began to walk from the room when the Lord said, go back. I knew then that I would not be able to pull a trick on God. I began to remove items from the closet without being affected by the value or my love for them. The Lord let me keep going until I only had six or seven outfits left. I put them together to be given to Salvation Army. A few days later, God did the same thing with my perfume. I had a large collection and did not hesitate when the Lord directed me to give it away. I kept two bottles. I still do not collect perfume. I didn't need to be told to get rid of my jewelry. I gradually did it. I was totally sold out to God's will for my life. (Not perfect but being perfected.)

By this time, I was experiencing problems with paying for my student loan. I no longer had the income to continue making the payments. I was contacted by phone about my being in arrears. Can you imagine, borrowing money to go to college four years, double majoring? I prayed about being behind in the payments. So, when the call came, all I could do was to tell the truth. I said, "I am no longer working, and will never be working again as I am now a minister with a call from God. I don't know what to do about this debt, but I will never have a job where I will be making money to pay for this loan." There was a time of silence. Then the caller said, "I will make a note of what you said, I don't know what will be done about you being in arrears in making your payments." I never heard from them again. I thought my credit score would be affected, but it wasn't. All I can say is, God took care of it. I owe no unpaid debts and have as we always have had an excellent credit rating.

In addition to teaching the weekly day Bible study, I also taught during women's fellowship, which was reaching beyond our church, and had outreaches on the east coast. I traveled with Pastor Charles late wife, Carolyn to Philadelphia, Pennsylvania where we held Covenant women's conferences. I taught the word on that which I had experienced the greatest—intercessory prayer and walking by faith. It seemed as if I was on a speedway traveling at such a great speed that I questioned the Lord frequently, "Lord is this you?" Can I really do this? Believe me when I say that I did not desire or seek to do anything but to be a good Christian woman. We had many conferences, fellowships, and retreats at our local church where I was a part of the ministry staff, as I had been ordained by Pastor Charles and Pastor Carolyn.

We usually held our annual women's retreat at Arrowhead Springs Christian Conference Center. At the Wednesday night Bible study before the first one that I attended to minister, A pastor, who was a friend of Pastor Charles who was attending was called to the front to have a word. While he was speaking, he said, "The Lord wants to do something." He said, there is someone here that has been holding unforgiveness against someone, and the Lord wants you to let it go." He said, "sister, come up here." as he pointed to me. I was amazed that he was speaking about me, as I felt that I was not holding anything against anyone. I went up and he laid hands on me and led me in a forgiveness prayer. As I sat back down, I was not only embarrassed, but I was in a state of denial.

After the service, on the way home, I prayed to the Lord in tears, "Lord if I am holding unforgiveness against anyone, reveal it to me, I want to be free of this." Immediately, A name came to me and I burst into tears. The name was "Mike," and I immediately knew that the word that the minister spoke was true. My daughter Linda's ex-husband was the person I pronounced death on after he had an accident in the car that we had purchased for her when she graduated from high school and went to college. After one year of college, she married Mike. He was suffering from being in the Vietnam war, and after his recovery, he ended the marriage and took the car and was driving back to his hometown in Minnesota. He had a wreck in Barstow, California. He left the accident, the car and the financial responsibility which cost us thousands of dollars. I was so angry, (this was before my salvation) I pronounced death on him. After I became a believer, I no longer thought about it. God didn't forget! I cried out to the Lord to forgive me, and the weight lifted off of me. 1 John 1:9, *"If we confess our sins, he is faithful and just to forgive us our sins, and to cleanse us from all unrighteousness."* Thank God for His goodness and mercy, without which where would we be?

As I had prepared for the women's retreat, it seemed as if I was walking in a different level of the Spirit of God. My trust in God was at a new level. I was totally committed to the Lord and His Word. While I was away, JJ got saved and filled with the Holy spirit. When I called home there was such excitement about his finally coming into what God had called us into. He didn't feel a call on his life, and I didn't feel that I should pull him in because I didn't even know where God was taking me. I had begun to flow in the gifts of the Spirit—not only tongues and interpretation of tongues, but prophesy, the gifts of healing and deliverance. It was at the retreat first time the gift of seeing and knowing operated through me. In the Spirit, I saw Pastor Charles in the pulpit, ministering and I saw a man from the audience come down to confront him while he was ministering. I called him to warn him. I was not sure if this was from God, like I said, this was the first time that I had this experience in the natural. I was told that during the Sunday service a man came from the congregation and approached him, but the ushers had been put on alert and was able to stop him. This gift works in my life as the Spirit wills. One thing that I learned was that when the anointed presence of the Lord is in the midst, supernatural manifestations take place. When his presence is not there, our flesh is in control, and guess who wins?

One thing that God did that was hard for me to understand at the time was to send me into the Old Testament to study. It was difficult for two reasons. One was after being a Catholic and being indoctrinated in Bible history and very little New Testament teaching, my confession was, "I've read it already." The second reason is, I fell in love with Jesus as I walked with Him supernaturally through the gospels, and became a woman of faith through the teaching of the epistles. As I tried continually to evade the study of the Old Testament, it seemed as if I was not getting what I needed from the New Testament, it seemed as if the New Testament was not giving me what I was getting before.

Finally, I made myself settle down and get into the Old Testament. It's amazing how when you move to obey the Lord, He opens your understanding of His plan. The Spirit of the Lord revealed to me that I only knew one side of God—the mercy side, but I needed to know the other side of our God. How could I teach others about a God that I only partially knew? So, as I went through the Old Testament, I saw the judgement side of God, the God who does not change, the God who judged the Israelites and gave to them according to their righteousness and obedience to Him. I realized that I needed to see this side of God and what He commanded in the Old Testament. That when Jesus came, died and arose again, He made it possible to keep God's commandments and be the people God commanded the Israelites to be. I saw that when we do not keep His commandments, if we don't repent and change our ways (a benefit of the cross) that what God proclaimed upon His people then will come upon us. It is necessary to know the one you will be journeying with— spending every moment of your life traveling the path He has placed you on.

It is a good thing that God does not give up on us as we travel the journey, expecting God to follow us instead of our following the path He has set before us. By now, my life was consumed with being in the presence of the Lord in intercessory prayer. I had reached a place in my prayer time that I was having so many supernatural experiences, I was reluctant to talk with anyone about them. I heard no one else speaking of similar experiences.

I had gotten Kenneth Hagin's book on prayer and the different kinds of prayer which helped some, but there were many questions unanswered about the experiences I was having. I would hear of flakey intercessors (the term was not commonly used at that time), doing weird things and pastors shutting down the prayer in their churches. So, when I was praying with the groups, I would quench the Spirit of God, going home to finish praying through. God was bringing prayer to the church that they had not experienced before. There was a world-wide intercessory prayer explosion going forth. Many pastors didn't want it in their churches. They didn't understand it and thought it was the flesh of the people involved which were mostly women.

God always has a plan in which we are brought into the place He wants us to be when He wants to correct and direct us. I heard about a women's conference that was going to be held at the University of Redlands Campus that had sessions on Intercessory prayer. It was a three-day conference, with nearby hotels available, if needed. As I tell people even now, I will travel to the ends of the earth to be in the presence of God. JJ agreed for me to go. I know now that this part of the journey of my life cleared the path for the rest of the journey. The Women of The Word Conference was powerful. It was filled with women who like me, were experiencing spiritual movements that they found no one to discuss with. Billie

Adams was the minister who was the director. She was a powerfully anointed woman whom God used mightily during the conference. But when I went into the meeting where prayer was being taught, I knew that this was why I was there. Bobbie Jean Merck, who taught the seminar on intercessory prayer taught on the things that I had been experiencing. I was so relieved to learn that it was God who was moving in my life. After each session, I would speak with others who had not understood what was going on in their prayer life either.

Perhaps you're wondering, what kind of things were happening? Well, things such as being moved to another scene as you are praying, experiencing seeing things before they happened and praying and seeing a different outcome than what would be presented to you to pray about. To see people on death beds raised up—people behind the gates of hell, being taken to nations, to see giant serpents filling church sanctuaries (satanic) and others that I will speak of as we continue.

The Lord was bringing people into my life to help me not resist Him as He moved me to do or speak something. One of the things He had to free me from, and it happened at the Women of the Word Conference was the denominational tradition that God did not call women to preach or to hold leadership positions in the church. I witnessed God using these women in every facet of ministry. I saw women being set free from all manner of bondage. Traditions can be bondage, and I could not continue the journey set before me until the old chains had fallen off. Bobbie Jean Merck laid hands on those who went up. I ran to the front. As she laid hands on me, the spirit of travail came upon me and others who went forward. The service ended with a powerful intercessory prayer session.

Every time God has added to the church and to the lives of the believer, there is the tendency to forsake what He has already added to you. God does not have anything He puts in our lives that becomes obsolete or made useless because of a new impartation. Everything He imparts to us is necessary for the journey He has set us on. Every new thing He would bring into my life was that which added to my ability to be successful on my journey. After the conference, the Lord blessed me to journey with Billie Adams, and other ministers to Israel, Greece, and Egypt. This made the journey with Jesus even more profound, not only did I walk in the Spirit with Jesus, but now I was walking the paths in the natural that He walked. Solidifying His life in me and my heart. Having a service in the Garden of Gethsemane, standing at the tomb of His resurrection and being baptized in the Jordan River. I became so divinely connected to Our Lord and Savior; I will never be the person that I use to be.

From that point, I began to be mentored by Bobbie

Jean Merck, following her to Santa Barbara where she frequently held prayer Seminars, to Washington D.C. for prayer for the nation and leaders, frequently to Houston for conferences, to Atlanta which was near her ministry home. God used her to cause me to be permanently established as a prayer warrior. Even though I was thought to be a weird woman, I no longer apologized for being the person that God was making me into. As intercessory prayer became a factor in the lives of Christians, the church could no longer ignore what God was doing.

Within months after the Women of the Word conference, another God sent prayer conference was scheduled at the Los Angeles Convention Center. This one was called "The Secrets of Intercession." There was a prayer explosion in the churches, and many pastors were not the participants. They did not understand it and didn't know how to differentiate the real from the abuse. It was a Holy Spirit anointed meeting with pastors getting understanding of what was taking place in their churches and becoming participants of this move of God. My pastor, Rev. Charles was in attendance. The reality of the fact that nothing of God takes place in the earth without prayer going forth. II Chron 7:14-15, *"If my people, which are called by my name, shall humble themselves, and pray, and seek my face, and turn from their wicked ways; then will I hear from heaven, and will forgive their sin, and will heal their land. 15 Now mine eyes shall be open, and mine ears attend unto the prayer that is made in this place."*

For me, this gave me greater understanding of what God was doing in me, but it began to open doors for me to teach others what God was teaching me. God never opens a door on the journey before you're ready to walk through it. During many prayer seminars, the Lord would show me a stage or platform in a setting with thousands of people in chairs attentive to the action on the platform. I never saw who it was on the stage, but now I know that person was me. My journey with the Lord would take me to this place not just a place, but many places. God in His wisdom does not reveal His plan to us before we can handle it and be responsible for our obedience or disobedience to His call, a humble beginning.

The beginning path of my journey with the Lord started in my home church. I taught the women's fellowship on intercessory prayer on Sunday evenings. I taught at our women's retreat and women's conferences. Always teaching that which God perfected in me—not going into areas that I did not have the anointing yet to teach. The Lord then began to open doors to go outside of the church to teach at other venues. My first journey away from my church directed by Pastor Charles, who had a distant relative in the Santa Barbara area who pastored a small church. I ministered a two-day seminar there. During this time, it was as if I was in a Holy Ghost school, some steps were productive, some were not. I learned that the non-productive steps were those that I had taken that were not ordered of the Lord. I remember accepting a speaking engagement in San Diego, given by a woman of God who had a women's ministry in a denominational church. I prepared myself by studying and praying. When I got there, I found out it was a time of paying homage to women who had made great achievement's by getting degrees in education, masters and doctorates and other recognitions. I had been so far removed from this by the Lord, that when I finally did get up to speak, my first words were, "I'm Denotra Johnson and the only degree that I hold that means anything to me is the BA degree (Born Again) that I have from the Kingdom of God." I taught on putting things in proper perspective as far as the Lord was concerned.

Each message I taught, or even now when I teach, it is for me first, and while I was studying, the Lord is ministering to me on the word that I am studying. Another thing I appreciate about the Lord, He won't permit me to step out, to teach anything before it is reality in my life. Certainly not faking it until you make it. I was never invited to minister at the San Diego ministry again. The Lord taught me early that I was not in control, that I must acknowledge Him in all things. Prov. 3:6, *In all thy ways acknowledge him, and he shall direct thy paths.*

A lesson came as correction from the Lord concerning my attitude. I was asked at the church to go in and help teach in Children's Church. My reply was, "I was not called by God to teach children." Well, within a few weeks, the Lord spoke to me (not audibly) that I was to go to the neighborhood park and teach a children's Bible study there. God's plan is to prepare us for the journey not by making things fit our desires, but by perfecting us so that His will would be done in the earth. Even knowing the voice of God, we try to get Him to change the path He has established before the foundation of the world was laid. I knew that I wasn't going to change God's mind, so I began to try to keep from happening what God said I was to do.

I had personal contact with the people in the county supervisor's office, so I called one of the people I knew and asked, "Is it legal to teach a Bible study to the children in the park while they're being served the free lunches?" In our ignorance, we try to block what God wants to do. Well, he said, "No you can't, but you can take a few kids, put them on a blanket and teach them and whoever comes to the blanket can be a part of it because you didn't go to them. They came to you while you were teaching the ones you brought to the park." After a while we're going to stop trying to outsmart God. So, I took my granddaughter Leslie and my grandson Justin and eight children who knew them came to the blanket and participated in the Bible study the first day. That summer, ninety-six children participated and received Jesus, not all on the same days.

In the evening of the last day of the free lunches, I invited the parents to come and have hot dogs, chips, and punch with all the children. None of this was paid for by anyone but me. The Lord was beginning to show me that there would be times that I would have to truly walk by faith. Pastor Charles was there to witness the miracle working power of God. I'm convinced that when we do not obey God, our journey is altered, and not by God. Jer. 29:11-12 (KJV), *"For I know the thoughts that I think toward you, saith the Lord, thoughts of peace, and not of evil, to give you an expected end. 12 Then shall ye call upon me, and ye shall go and pray unto me, and I will hearken unto you."* I went back the next year with similar results, not because God said to do it, but I saw the fruit produced for the kingdom of God and my attitude was changed.

After this happened, I became more aware of what God was trying to teach me, that I could not lock myself into what I felt was fitting for me to do. God was preparing me for multitudes of things that I didn't feel was right for me to do. But I continually prayed, "Thy will be done in my life." It is amazing how we can say things to God when we pray such as "thy will be done" and when He reveals His will to us for our lives, we try to either talk God out of His will or deny that God is in the plan. The journey that we are on is a learning experience as I was on a path that I never walked or even thought that I would walk.

Pastor Charles developed a neighborhood door to door outreach in Pomona where the church was located. Several things took place that helped me to hear and obey the leading of the Lord at all costs, regardless of the opinions of others. First, as I was dressing for the Saturday outreach to neighborhoods, I put on pants and a shirt. As I put my hands on the doorknob ready to do the Lord's work of evangelizing the community, I heard in my spirit, "Put on a dress." I thought it was just a crazy thought I had. But as I put my hands back on the doorknob again, I heard it again, but this time it was more authoritative. I didn't understand it, but I knew it was not my mind. So, I went back in and changed into a skirt and blouse. We went from house to house, sharing Jesus with many receptive people. Some did not receive us. In one house the husband and wife let us come in and share Jesus with them. They accepted the Lord, and when we were leaving, as we came out of the house, a woman was coming up the driveway. She had a walker. The Lord said, "Pray for her." I asked her if we could pray for her and she looked at me, then said, "Yes." We prayed for God to heal her. The power of God fell on her, she began to pray in tongues, and she lifted up the walker and was praising the Lord loudly. This woman was a traditional Pentecostal Christian. From a church that believed that Christian women did not wear pants. I understood why the Lord directed me to put on a dress. He knew that this woman would be on our path, and He wanted to heal her and if I was in pants, she would not have received from me anything I offered her. This taught me that we must be sensitive to the natural environment as we do the work of the Lord.

The second experience was another time when my friend, Gail and I were knocking on doors together, when we were invited into an apartment by a man. I don't know what he thought we were there for, but he invited us to sit down. And when I began to talk about the Lord and salvation, He got up, his face was filled with a violent response. He walked over to the door, opened it and said, "Get out." I didn't realize he was talking to us, as his attitude had changed so. So, he said it again, and this time there was violence in his tone. We got up and left immediately. He slammed the door behind us. This man was a Muslim, and this was a time when there was much violence towards those who were not in agreement with their doctrine. The Lord was protecting us in our ignorance.

The Lord began to give me dreams and visions that I did not understand. I didn't discuss them with anyone. I didn't want to be considered weird or crazy. As I look back now, I understand that God was mapping out the journey that I would be taking, where it was taking me and how I would get to the destination He had mapped out for my life. As I moved into an area of ministry, I would be given the connection of the dream or vision and where I was. Besides seeing multitudes of people before me in many different settings, I once found myself on a hill looking down into a valley when suddenly a great storm swept through, blowing all the life off the trees. As the wind blew, I found myself in the valley picking up the leaves and putting them in a container. It seemed as if I would never be able to recover the destruction of the storm, but I kept picking them up and putting them in the safe place so they would not be lost. When the vision ended, I knew that this was not my mind. I just determined that if this was God and I did not know what it meant, when the time came, God would reveal it to me.

One Sunday morning during the service, while the praise team was ministering the anointing was so strong and the presence of God was so evident it seemed as if we would be lifted up into heaven. All of a sudden, I felt myself being lifted up. I looked around me, but I was not standing in the front row of the church any more. I was ascending upward. I didn't know what was happening, but I thought I was going to heaven, it was so peaceful, I was not afraid. I could still hear the praise from the church. Suddenly, I stopped ascending and began to descend. There was nothing to see around me, I just kept going down and down. Suddenly, I stopped going down and my feet were on a solid foundation. As my eyes opened wide, I was standing in front of an iron fence with a wide gate which I could see through. I now know that I was standing at the gates of hell. As I focused on what was before me, I saw inside this humongous structure which seemed to have no boundaries. But what was taking place inside shook me in a way that is indescribable. There were multitudes of people, men and women who were running and screaming while being chased and tormented by what I now know were demons. They were being assaulted, and attacked, but then my ears popped open, and I could hear the praise team from the church. But then I heard the heavenly angels singing with them. And I knew this was more tortuous for the residents of hell than what the demons were doing to them. It seemed that I was there for a long period of time, but when I began to ascend and was suddenly back in the place where I was before I was taken, the praise team was just finishing the song they were singing when I ascended. This experience had such an effect on me, as I could not tell anyone because I did not want to be called a crazy woman. But I knew as I know now that it was God showing me that hell is real, and my ministry was to keep as many from ending up there as possible. This caused me to put the call on my life before anything else.

Our Pastors, Charles and Carolyn Harrell had connections with a great Pastor from Nigeria, Dr. Benson Idahosa who pastored many churches in that country. Those churches were having a women's conference and Pastor Carolyn was invited to be a speaker. Pastor JJ said that I could attend even though I was not going to be part of the ministry team, I was excited about being in the midst of an international Women's Conference. So, I began to make plans to follow them to Nigeria. I got my passport and my reservations, without telling Pastor Charles that I was going to be there. I just had the desire to go to witness what God was doing in other parts of the world. I didn't seek the Lord as to whether or not this was in His plan for me. But I soon found out that God had another plan.

As I was getting everything together, I went to a neighborhood shopping center where I noticed a new jewelry store in the center. I decided to go in to look around. As I walked around, I saw a Bible on the counter. The lady behind the counter was a Pilipino with a smile on her face as she greeted me. I asked her if she was a Christian and she replied, "Yes, I am." We began to talk about the Lord. She said she was a Baptist but was excited to have someone to talk to about the Lord. As I spent more and more time with her God was divinely connecting us. Through her, I met other Pilipino people. During this time, I got information that Marilyn Hickey, the powerful evangelist and teacher of the word whom I had helped our church plan a meeting for in Anaheim, California, was planning a ministry trip to the Philippines. Since I had been connected to the Pilipino people through my new friend, I was interested. But I knew that I could not go to both Africa and the Philippines. So, I began to fast and seek the Lord as to which way I should go. My husband, JJ did not want to go, but agreed for me to go whichever way the Lord led me. After much prayer and fasting, Africa did not have the drawing power that I sensed before.

I sent for more information on Marilyn Hickey's ministry trip to the Philippines. I knew within me that God was involved in my decision. I had no idea that this was the beginning of a long journey that would last twelve years and would take me into many other countries. After much prayer and fasting, I knew the Lord was ordering my steps. The Philippine trip was God's plan for me to take. My mother decided to go with me as she had traveled out of the country, ministering mostly in the Islands and South America. I was excited because I knew that God was at the center of this trip. All of my local Pilipino friends had things to send to their families. So, before I got there, I was connected to three pastors in the Manila area. I had connections with God's people before I even got there. My mother and I decided that we would go a week before the group's departure.

Looking back now, I see how easy it is to take credit for something that works out so well.

We were to stay at the Manilla Hotel, the hotel that housed General MacArthur during World War II. It was still dedicated to him with his facilities held intact. But when we got there, one of our contacts, a pastor who had a Bible college and church in a nearby village invited us to stay at the facility. We delivered to him what was sent by his family. We slept in the dormitory and had meals with Pastor Ormeo and his wife at their house on the same property. The church was located there also. They were very cordial and thankful for the packages and cash that I delivered to them. While with them, my mother and I rode the jeepneys to downtown Manilla where there is a large park and gathering place where homeless and others spent their time during the day. As we got there, we saw thousands wandering around the area. Some were homeless, including children without adult supervision. Others were there picnicking. We passed out flyers, witnessed to hundreds and led many to the Lord. There were some who were hostile, cultish and anti-Christ. One very belligerent man, who confronted us by saying, "Instead of handing out those papers why don't you bring apples for the children, most of them have never eaten one." The Lord protected us as we spent the whole day there. We rode the jeepney back to the dormitory which was about an hour's trip.

The next day, another pastor to whom we brought a package from his aunt in West Covina, California, Pastor Jude Garcia, came to Pastor Ormeo's house to see us and get the items sent to him. He was different from Pastor Ormeo as his demeanor was different. At that time, I did not know that it had anything to do with him being spirit filled. But he was very kind and respectful of the position we occupied. He was happy to receive the delivery and invited me to come and minister at his church on Friday night. I accepted, not knowing what to expect. I had not had any contact with any of the students when the next day the one who was the pastor's assistant volunteered to take mother and me to downtown Manila where there were many outdoor shopping centers where we shopped and handed out flyers.

After we returned to the dormitory, we dressed for the Friday night service at Pastor Jude's church. I say church because I didn't know that his church was just being established, and I was the speaker of the first service of Cross Tower Christian Center. The service was held outside in Pastor Jude's father's business yard. It was on a very busy street with folding chairs accommodating around a hundred people. After I ministered the word (The ministry of the Holy Spirit) many people came forth to receive the Lord, being slain in the spirit. Multitudes of people passing by stopped to watch, some even on the roof of buildings looking on. The jeepney's passing by slowed to see what was going on. It was a powerful divine intervention of the Holy Spirit. Multitudes received the infilling of the Holy Spirit. I prayed for everyone there, with multitudes lying on the asphalt of the business yard. Occasionally, I still peruse my collection of pictures of the service, as one of the men used my camera to take them. It was a real experience for me as it was my first service outside of the United States. The anointing was different from what I had experienced in the churches I had ministered in. The people were hungry for the presence of God. This was a divine connection that continued for many trips to their church. This connection still exists as Pastor Jude started a church in Southern California where I minister occasionally.

On the Sunday following Pastor Jude's Friday night service, I was asked to come to the Church of Pastor Ormeo. I knew it was a Baptist Church, but I didn't know what to expect. I soon found out. I was not warmly accepted, first because of being a woman, as I was asked, don't they have any men ministers in America? And because of the message of the ministry of the Holy Spirit, I was not treated too well. The women even were not social after the service. We were to leave for the hotel in Manilla to connect with Marilyn Hickey and the other ministers the next day. We were prayerfully excited, knowing that I would begin to be mentored for what the

Lord had for me to do. When we got to the hotel, all of the group of twenty-six of us met, greeted each other and had prayer together and was given a schedule. It was a busy time of ministry.

We had conferences outdoors in poor communities where people lived in huts, tents, and brush buildings. At one poor community there were over two thousand people standing, waiting for us to arrive. There was a flatbed long trailer on which we were standing as Marilyn ministered the word. Afterwards, we step down and as directed by Marilyn, we lined up in front of the vehicle so that the people who needed and wanted prayer could line up in front of each one of us. which was next to their houses, huts, and tents.

We prayed for and laid hands on multitudes of people. We saw miracles in front of us multitudes of times. The supernatural power of God was manifested. Crippled people were walking, growths were erased. We, as ministers, were astounded at the availability of God's healing and delivering anointing we were experiencing. When we were back at the hotel later, we discussed the people we had prayed for, and it seemed as if God anointed each of us for a specific healing need. I know that the majority of people I laid hands on were healed of TB and Leprosy. We were so excited about what God was doing. Each day, we went to a different area to minister. The people came out in great numbers, hungry for the word and the presence of God. We went to the church that Lester Sumrall had established where Marilyn ministered. That was a real powerful time of gathering with our group.

I had one more package to deliver. The pastor came to the hotel to meet me. He was Pastor Vic Andaya, a former Pilipino movie star, drug smuggler and a real tough man. He had gotten saved after living a real rough life. He was not an easy man to contend with. But the Lord gave me favor with him. He invited me to come to his church to minister. I accepted the invitation. I did not know what denomination it was, but the message the Lord had given me to take to the people was the ministry of the Holy Spirit and prayer. He came for mother and me and I found that his church was in the same area that he had served Satan in. When he came to the Lord, all the people he controlled harshly came after him. He had been attacked, his church vandalized, and many threats were made against him. But he established his church in that community called Las Pinas. They were very friendly and accepting. I ministered the message, but as I was teaching, I felt that this was all new to them. Afterwards, I prayed for many to be healed and some accepted the Lord. When I offered to minister the Holy Spirit to anyone who desired, no one responded. It amazed me that it seemed as if this was all new to them. Even pastor Vic's wife and son and daughter seemed to be amazed as what I was teaching. I had done what the Lord gave me to give them not knowing that this also was a Baptist Church. Afterwards he took us back to the hotel and was very kind to us.

The next day, we flew into Singapore where we checked in at the hotel and my mother and I went out to pass out tracs and minister to people on the street. That was not my ministry, but my mother was anointed for this kind of ministry. I just supported her and we prayed for some. Singapore was kind of an upscale country with many restrictions. It was like spotless everywhere we went. The next day Marilyn was scheduled to minister at a gathering where we all went. She was welcomed and received with honor. Each day of ministry found mother and I on the streets. I was kind of wanting to shop, so another woman stayed with her one day. She stood on the sidewalks with boldness talking to people about the Lord. We were there four days before we flew back to Manila where we flew back home from. It was a powerful learning experience. This is where the Lord revealed the meaning of the vision that I had of the storm that was blowing leaves off the trees and away. It was when I saw myself picking up the leaves and putting them in a container that the revelation came to me that I was the evangelist that rescued the lost and put them in the place God built for them, the Church. When that was revealed to me, I wept. God is awesome!! But I had a problem accepting the fact that God had called me to stand in the position of an evangelist, especially since I knew so many men that could fill the position. I won't say that I wasn't shaken, even though I had experienced the miracle working power of God. I didn't feel that I was worthy to stand in that position. I said to the Lord many times, "Lord, I am a woman" as if He had made a mistake. The Lord reminded me of what happened when Balaam wanted to disobey Him, God used a donkey to bring him into submission. (Numbers 22:20-38). I realized that I was acting as if He had made a mistake. But as long as I obeyed, God did not rebuke me but gave me peace.

On the flight home, we stopped in Honolulu, Hawaii where a friend of my mother was pastoring a church which her husband had established before he passed away. She was now overseer but was controlled by the deacons. I had no knowledge of any of this. But she asked me if I would minister at the Sunday night service, which I agreed to do. This was a very difficult experience as when I got up front, I was surrounded by the deacons. I didn't know how to handle this. I was led to start my sermon with prayer, and then ask everyone to please be seated as I didn't want any distraction from the sermon the Lord had given me. The deacons reluctantly sat down. The message was basically the same as the one that I carried to the Philippines, about the Holy Spirit. There was an acceptive response as they followed the word in the Bible. Afterwards, I gave the alter call then asked if there was anyone who needed prayer. Mostly women came up, only several men. But the deacons all came and stood around me. I still don't know what they expected. I didn't either. But the Holy Spirit moved upon me and the anointing for healing was great. Each person that I laid hands on went out in the Spirit. The deacons did not expect this but moved to the back of those receiving prayer to catch them to prevent any harm as them went out in the Spirit. Many were healed, and when service was over, the deacons were more responsive to me. I left praising the Lord for what He had done.

When I got home, I began to receive letters from many of the people that I had ministered to. This gave me peace about the call on my life. I made a commitment to return to the Philippines the next year. But during the year, the Lord removed me from Walnut Faith Center and Pastor Charles Harrell. I questioned the reason, and I was shown that my place there was an associate pastor and that is not what He had planned for me. The departure was not a pleasant one. I had developed such a close relationship with the staff and members. So much gossip and bitterness prevailed because of my departure, the Lord sent me into Los Angeles to connect with a church of a pastor that I had little connection with. I obeyed and my wonderful husband, JJ agreed, and so for almost a year, we were a part of the Power of Love Christian Fellowship in Los Angeles, which was thirty-nine miles away from where we lived.

We were blessed with Pastor Edward Turner's leadership. I ministered there when I was asked, but I knew that this was a temporary situation to keep anyone from leaving Walnut Faith Center to follow me for we form connections as we minister to the members of the church. I was continually ministering in churches when the Lord led me to begin to hold prayer conferences in the San Gabriel Valley area of Los Angeles County. The conferences were held at the Covina Bowl Bowling Center's conference room. The attendance was amazing. There were so many women that felt that they were called to be intercessors who needed teaching on what God had called them to do. The presence of the Lord was greatly manifested at these meetings which were held monthly. We had guest speakers who were anointed prayer warriors. I did this for two years.

After a period of time, we were asked to become a part of a new church that was forming in Pomona, California by Pastors James and Saundra O'Neal. We agreed to be a part of the church when we were available as we were traveling. JJ was not always able to be with me in the field as he was still working. So, the Lord connected me with Gail Green, who was with me on the next trip to the Philippines. This trip was not just for the Philippines, as we also went to Hong Kong and China. This was a trip that was dangerous as we were carrying Bibles in our suitcases and on our bodies. The Philippine connection was powerful. I ministered at Pastor Jude Garcia and Vic Andaya's churches again. I made connection with a pastor who had been a student at Pastor Ormeo's Bible college but was now pastoring a church on the island of Negros Occidental. Before I left, I connected with an orphanage and supplied food and clothes to the children. I also gave apples to the children. The time spent there was anointed, with many spiritual connections made. I was asked to come back again.

From there we move on to Hong Kong which was our entry path into China. This was a dangerous trip as we didn't know how to conduct ourselves safely. I put myself in a place of danger on the train as there were many Chinese soldiers aboard. With my camera, I stood up and looking back toward the soldiers, I began to take pictures. A uniformed man came up to me and was speaking in Chinese. Our guide, who was a young Chinese college student who was connected with the group of Christian students who were assisting us with the delivery of the Bibles, stood up and told the officer that I was ignorant of the rules in the country and that he would see that this did not happen again. So, I was not arrested as I could have been. On the way through the inspection before entering, our suitcases were on the conveyer to be inspected. As I was in line, a soldier came to me speaking Chinese, directing me to follow him with my suitcase. You can imagine the fear that gripped me since I was the only black person in the group.

As I followed him, he took me into a room and motioned for me to sit down on a sofa as he was holding my visa and passport. I sat with my suitcase in front of me. He began to speak to me in Chinese. I didn't know what he was saying, but the words came to me what to say. So, I said, "tourist." He continued asking me something, and I continued to say, "tourist." He ceased talking and just kept staring at me. I was so nervous, I thought I was going to be searched. He then stood up and handed me my passport and visa and waited for me to stand. But I couldn't because the Bibles on my body had shifted. He waited, looking at me. It came to me to grab the top of my luggage which was in front of me and push myself up. I know it was the Lord directing me. I did so, and he escorted me from the room. I still had to let my suitcase which was lined with Bibles go through the inspection. Praise God, it passed through without any problem. As I came to the inside of the China wall, everyone was waiting for me, praying that I would be released.

When we arrived in the town where we were to deliver the Bibles, we took a while to connect with everyone while waiting for the guide who would take us to the drop off place. It was a nervous time as we did not know who the guide would be. There was some panicking, as just above the place where we were gathered, multitudes of Chinese soldiers were gathered. There were great fences surrounding the entry into the city. Military weapons were on the fences with soldiers manning them. After waiting awhile, a young man walked by and said, "follow me." We walked a great distance into an area that was not heavily inhabited, and he led us into a house. We were told to place the Bibles on a large table. We had to remove the Bibles from our bodies without considering privacy. And as we removed them, they were being packaged up in two's and sent out by students. After we had released the Bibles, we went to a department store and shopped a bit. Then we went on a cruise ship for a relaxing trip, which I needed. This was a very learning experience, as I saw that the call on my life was not a call for fame or fortune, but in some cases, it would be life threatening. The cruise was not joyful to me, as we went by many cities that I knew people needed to hear about the Lord Jesus Christ, and after almost losing my life, I decided that I wanted my life to count for something.

When I arrived back home, I did not immediately relay the China experience to anyone. I kind of had the idea that if JJ knew about it, he would not be so much in agreement with the call on my life. So, I continued to minister at the Covina Bowl, teaching on prayer and commitment. The door was opened for me to minister at a women's retreat in Prescott, Arizona, given by my niece, Beverly Benton who had a women's outreach ministry. It was a powerful time of women being prepared for God's work. During the retreat several of the women asked me if I would bring to Phoenix what I was teaching there. When I got home, I began to pray about the request. I felt the Lord's directing me to do so, not realizing that I would be doing the conferences there every year for ten years. This was a time of powerfully anointed ministry. Other women ministers came as guest speakers from all over the United States.

The overseas ministry continued. I went back to the Philippines each year, making seven more trips. The Lord opened the door in several additional Islands of the Philippines. One of my American Pilipino friends had a sister living on the Isle of Ilo Ilo, and since I had an engagement on the island of Negros Occidental. I planned both trips together. Taking a break from the Manilla ministry, my friend Gail accompanied me as we flew to the Island of Negros where we observed the church that JJ and I had supported to help build. The pastor was the young man who assisted us at Pastor Ormeo's Bible school, accompanying us into Manilla on several occasions. He was no longer a student, but now a Pastor. We spent several nights there and then took a boat to the Island of Ilo Ilo where we were greeted by the sisters of my friend. It was an interesting time. The sisters were not knowledgeable of the things of God but were devout Catholics, so it was not an easy task of ministering to them. They were pretty social and well known and respected on the island. I gave them the word of God concerning salvation and prayed for them and their salvation. We had lunch with them and proceeded to the airport to go back to Manilla.

The ministry expanded as another church was opened to me ministering to the congregation on a Sunday morning during another trip. The church was Jesus Reigns Christian Center in Manilla. The pastors were Rev. Vincent and Lagaya Javier. This was a very large church being held in a four story commercial building. As I was entering the building, I had to take an elevator to the third floor. The presence of the Lord was great as the praise singers ministered. As I delivered the message of salvation and the Holy Spirit's ministry, multitudes of the congregation came forward to be filled with the Holy Spirit and to be healed. As I was ministering, I noticed activity throughout the building, but as I was under the anointing I didn't concentrate on the surroundings. Many were filled with the Holy Spirit and healed by God. From time to time, I look at the pictures that were taken during the service, But I only found out after the service was over that the fire department was moving throughout the whole building because of the smoke permeating the building. I could have told them that it was the glory of

God, as I knew that I was surrounded by the presence of God during the service. They found no reason for the smoke like atmosphere!

This movement of God divinely connected me to this church and the pastors. During this trip I was taken by the pastors to the men's prison where I ministered to a large group of prisoners. Many gave their lives to the Lord, and many came up to receive prayer for physical and emotional problems. This was the same prison that Lester Sumrall talked about a miracle that took place when he ministered there. On my next trip, I ministered at all of my church connections and went back to the prison. This time the prison had built a sanctuary where I ministered. As we were leaving, one of the guards called to me and said that one of the prisoners wanted to speak to me. Since I had already signed out, he brought the man to the fence. He was a black man. I was shocked to see him in a Philipino prison. He asked me to do him a favor. It seemed he was the son of a military man who had been stationed in Manilla. His father was no longer in the military and lived in northern California. The son had been in this prison for thirteen years. I did not ask what he did to get there. He wanted me to call his father when I got home and ask him to communicate with him. He had had no connection with him since he had been imprisoned. He gave me his information. When I got home, I wrote the father a letter. I don't know how it turned out. I did what I promised him I would do.

Through this church, I was asked to minister at a retreat of college students. This was in a large facility in a densely populated town. There were hundreds of male and female students. They were very receptive which made the way for a move of the Holy Spirit. Many received the Lord and were filled with the Holy Spirit. I did not stay over night as I had another ministry appointment early the next day. I was also asked to travel with the pastor and a group of ministers to a community where survivors of a volcano eruption had been relocated. This eruption was a violent one, killing many people who no one even knew existed on that mountain. There were around one hundred men, women and children living in cabins the church had built. The church brought food, clothing and medical supplies to the community. I was able to minister to them and pray for them. They did not speak English, so a translator was used. This was the first time that I had to have a translator in the Philippines. This was a very humbling experience to encounter people no one knew even existed, finding out about them in a tragic experience. The humility and care of people this church showed made me understand one of the purposes of God's church today.

My last trip to the Philippines was a time of connecting with those the Lord had brought into my life to minister to. In addition to the churches, I was taken by a pastor to a group of people who lived on a stretch of rocks that led onto the South China Sea. The pastors had an outreach there. They brought with us a group of medical students and physicians. It was a long walk on the rocks to get to the place where a group of people were gathered. On the way to them you could see ocean water and big rats moving through the rocks. When we reached the group that was gathered, tables were set up. I was told that I was to minister to the people before the people were given medical help. The people were very receptive, and I prayed for those who had issues. Afterwards, medical and dental treatment took place. Medicines that had been donated to the church was distributed. When we had finished the ministry, the pastor told me that someone had prepared lunch and wanted me to come to their house to eat with them. I really didn't want to accept because the living quarters were tents and little shacks. I really didn't want to accept, but the Lord would not release me from this. So, I went into the hut, and on the ground was a tablecloth with several plates and food containers. As they greeted me, they fixed a plate for me and handed it to me. They were very friendly and loving. They poured me soda from a container. I really didn't want to eat the food, but I had to. The only help was the soda that I used to wash down the food that I couldn't swallow without it.

I had no idea that this was the last of my seven trips

to the Philippines. On the day before my departure, Pastor Vic Andaya came to the hotel to take me to the military base where I was to baptize a group of people in the swimming pool there. There were around twenty-five people waiting. It was a very anointed time of fulfilling the word of God in baptizing. After the service was over, Pastor Vic asked me if I would go to the Base Commanding Officers house on the base and pray for him as he was ill. I was amazed at God opening the door for me to be able to minister to famous people of authority. As usual, when I left the Philippines, I thanked the Lord for manifesting Himself to the people of that country. I still have connections with some of the ministers and their congregation.

The journey was not over as the door opened for me to go into Jamaica to hold a women's convention at the church of Pastors Stoney and Evelyn Fairweather. They pastored four churches and had a Bible college there. three times I took groups of approximately twenty people with me. JJ accompanied me on two of the trips. We always took clothes, toys, and Bibles for the women and children. The churches were filled with the presence of God. Many people were healed, saved, and delivered. One woman who was demon possessed was disturbing the service on our first trip. She was sitting on the front row. I asked my mother and another of our group to take her to the back room and pray for her. After the service was over, several of the women went with me to see what was happening. The woman was lying on the floor with my mother laying hands on her and commanding the demons to come out of her. As she was being set free, she cried out, "I want my spirits back." The Lord said to me, "Let her go." So, we ceased praying for her and she got up and walked out of the door. Then the Lord said to me, tell the pastors not to permit her to occupy that front seat again. I found out that she was a great financial supporter and used that to gain favor in the church.

On my last of the three ministry trips to Jamaica we had twenty people, with JJ, another Pastor and his assistant who was a musician with us. He had his instruments with him. The first two trips we stayed in cottages on the beach. On our third trip, as I was making reservations, the person I was speaking to on the phone said that because of our faithful service, they were giving us a private lodge which would accommodate all the women, and any men with us would be placed in a chalet a few blocks away. This was on a hilltop of a swanky community. I accepted it as I felt that God was rewarding us. The services were powerful, the women cane from all around. We rented a van that would carry all of us around during our time there. We hired a driver from the church, and we hired his sister who was to cook and clean for us. It seemed that this was going to be the greatest of all the trips to Jamaica, as everything seemed to be in order. The meetings were awesome. The spirit of God was moving in every service.

Although this was a woman's conference, men were there in a great number. We had brought with us, many dolls and toys for the children and clothes for the women. These were to be given out the night before we were to return home, After the third night service we returned back to our resort. The woman who was our cook had prepared a night snack for us. We were happy to have something to eat before going to bed. As we retired for the night, JJ was staying with me. I was awakened early the next morning, with the women telling me that we had been robbed. JJ and I jumped up and saw that everything in the room where we had put all the gifts was gone, including my purse which was on the nightstand beside our bed. We didn't know what to do, so we called Pastor Stoney. We saw that everything we brought with us was gone. The women lost nothing in their room. Just where JJ and I were sleeping and in the big room where all the valuable things we brought with us were. The woman who was our housekeeper and cook slept downstairs. She said she heard the people who were robbing us, but she did nothing. She said they were in the house for at least an hour. We walked around the building trying to figure out how this happened. I looked down the hill in the back of the building and saw my purse lying in the grass and weeds. I walked down there and saw that my purse had been defecated and urinated on and was empty.

When Pastor Stoney arrived, he was very upset. We called the police, but they never showed up. So, Pastor Stoney drove JJ and the men with him to the police station. The sergeant said that they already had caught the people who robbed us and had confiscated our material. When they asked if they could have the stolen merchandise back, they were told that they had to list it and they could pick it up the next day. When they went back the next day, half of the things were no longer there. They had disappeared from the police station. There was no way that we could fight with the law enforcers in their country. So, we had to just settle for what was left. I was able to stop payment on the checks in my accounts and cancel the credit cards. I was given a temporary American Express card to get us home. We were able to distribute the gifts that were left at the last service. Before we left Jamaica, we were warned that our trip had made us the victims of collusion. Those that were our helpers set us up. There was nothing that we said or did to reveal our vulnerability to robbery. We had been drugged with the food that we ate the night of the robbery causing us to be soundly asleep. This was our last ministry trip to Jamaica.

During the trips ministering in Jamaica the door was opened for me to join a group of ministers going into Russia right after the fall of Communism. I was really excited as it seemed as if the Lord was opening doors into countries that I intercede for daily. By now, the Lord had directed us to sell our home that was too big for the two of us and was costing too much maintain as we had a large swimming pool which we did not have time to use. So, before the trip to Russia, we sold the house and purchased a town house in Glendora, CA. JJ could not get off work to accompany me on the trip to Russia, which was planned by the California Christian TV station, TBN. This was an exciting trip as it took us into Moscow, St. Petersburg, and Kiev. The trip started out very shaky, as when we reached New York City, the plane that we were to take to Moscow had a mechanical problem, so we had to be in a hotel there until the next day. When we finally were settled on the plane, we knew this would be a very rocky flight. I knew no one on the plane. It was interesting watching the drinking and social gathering of those who I supposed to be Christians. When we reached Russia, the process of going through customs was very trying. Communism had just fallen, and the military and KGB were all over the airport. It took quite awhile to get into the country. The hotel we stayed at in Moscow was right across the road from the park where the communist army gathered and was frequently televised.

We had scheduled meetings in a large auditorium. We held three meetings there. It was an interesting time, as when we were praising the Lord, there were many young people who came out of their seats and were dancing. (worldly) When we ministered the word, it was so new to most of the people, and especially the ability to gather for a Christian meeting. So many of those attending came forward to receive the Lord and for prayer for healing. Each meeting was powerful. We were able to go to the hospitals where some of the children that were victims of the Chernobyl atomic explosion were. We were able to lay hands on them and pray for many of them. We were able to travel around, and sightsee. We even went to a church meeting where an American man was speaking. While we were in Moscow, they had a military gathering at the meeting place across the street from the hotel. Many of us went. We handed out tracts to many of them. I took lots of pictures of the gathering. It was a very poor time for Russia. The restaurants where we ate had a very poor quality of food. We basically stayed hungry the whole time there. This was prevailing throughout the country.

We flew to Kiev on a terrible plane. While we were in the air the flight was so bumpy that overhead luggage fell on many of us. We visited many sites that we had seen on T.V. We shopped and witnessed to multitudes of people who seemed to be receptive. We went to a church museum. It had all the interior things churches have, but no services were ever held there. It was a replica of what they felt was an American church. We met many people who were open to the gospel we were sharing with them. We prayed for many people who were in desperate situations. From there we flew on to St. Petersburg where we ministered to large groups of people who were hungry for change. Many were fearful as they had no idea of what was happening in their country. From there we flew back to Moscow. It was very cold for the first of May, and we were very hungry because of the shortage of good food. So, we got in line, which was two blocks long to get food at the McDonald's restaurant. It was the most food that we had eaten since we got there.

The next day we flew out of Russia. From there we stopped in Germany where I got off in order to fulfill a promise that I would come and minister. I now feel that this was not on God's plan for me, as it was not received, and I was not treated very well. I experienced racial prejudice as I had not since I had been traveling to carry the gospel to the world.

My next ministry trip to the nations came as Marilyn Hickey wrote me about an upcoming trip to minister at a church pastored by an African man in London, England. I was very excited as any time I traveled with Marilyn, there was always a mighty move of God. This trip was an exciting one. The meetings were so anointed. We laid hands on multitudes of people as the church was packed for each service. Each one of us was able to minister to the people. It was not a large group, but very committed and anointed ministers. We were able to see the country as I had never done before. We went to Buckingham Palace, and all the famous sites. The only thing that hindered us, as we traveled on the first of December, was the snow. As we had planned to go to a very large park to have an outdoor service, but there was a large group protesting something, and the law enforcement turned us away. But it was a very successful ministry trip.

Somehow, I felt that this was the last of my traveling to the nations. One reason I felt this way was because as we traveled to carry the gospel to the nations, we received no money from any church or anyone to help us pay for the travels. It was all financed as I withdrew my retirement funds from the county of Los Angeles where I had worked as a nurse, a secretary, and telephone operator. And from the Federal Government where I worked as an auditor for the Federal Tax office. That along with what JJ contributed financed all our ministry trips. Now it was used up, and I didn't know what God had planned. But I knew He had a plan.

As we were now ministering in retreats and local churches in addition to the Women's Conference in Phoenix, the Lord directed us to join Pastor Ken Cloudus at Community Christian Center in Covina, California, which was only a few miles from our townhouse. Divine connection with God is very important. JJ and I fit in very well with the congregation at our new church home.

One thing I learned was that God does not move without a purpose. The Lord spoke to me that I was to go to Mississippi. I did not even consider that this was God because of my memories of life there in my early years. He continually gave me directions, and finally, I told JJ, who had a negative experience there when he was in the military. His words to me were, "If the Lord is telling you to go, you'd better obey Him." He said, "I won't be going with you." So, I began to seek the Lord on how to do this. I contacted a cousin whom I had never met or had contact with, Patsy Hampton, who said I was welcome to stay with her while I was there. God is so awesome. The Spirit of God was with me in such a powerful way.

I flew into Jackson, Mississippi, and found that I had missed the last bus of the day to get to Philadelphia where Patsy was to meet me and drive me to Dekalb where she lived. So, I had to stay in a hotel there. It was a time that the Holy Spirit was upon me in a great way as the Lord was ministering strength and His love for my obedience to Him when I didn't know what was ahead. I didn't know what it was then, but I do now. I carried meetings there three years with the Lord pouring out His love and healing power. JJ was with me on the following trips. The big thing is, even if you don't know why God is directing you to move in a certain way, if you know it is what God is directing you to do, if you don't obey, you will find yourself standing still. I soon found out why I was there. I had carried the gospel to fourteen countries, but now I was to bring it to the place where I began. I met my relatives that I remembered, but most of them I had never seen or knew existed. They were Christians from many denominations. The Lord directed me to seek a place to bring meetings to Dekalb. In such a small town, everyone knew everyone. So, I was accepted, and a Pastor of a denominational Church said I could bring the meetings to his Church. This was not a Pentecostal church. I did this for three years and the acceptance of the Lord was great, with many lives changed. After the first visit, the Lord let me know that He had to bring my love back to the only place that I did not consider a loveable place or many loveable people because of past memories, even if they did not influence me in my love walk with Him.

Soon the Lord began to open doors in cities in Southern California to hold women's meetings and Bible studies. One bible study was in Hesperia, California which I held weekly at a young couple's home. People from the High Desert began to come until I became concerned that they were depending on me to be their spiritual leader. Without praying and seeking God, I was moved by my emotions and stopped holding the Bible study. I later found out how negatively this affected many of the attendees. Falling away from serving the Lord, leading to criminal activities, divorce and other demonic activities. I began to hold a Bible study at the Holiday Inn and a monthly women's conference in Victorville, California. I soon realized that Pastor Ken was mentoring me for traveling in a different direction for God.

In 1992 when JJ retired, the Lord gave us a desire to move to the High Desert. We did not do this rapidly because in 1986 we tried to relocate to Apple Valley. But it did not work out because of the distance JJ would have to travel to get to work and we wanted to be where God wanted us to be. But the notion did not go away. It became plain that the journey God has for me is taking us to the High Desert. As we prayed, we sought council from Pastor Ken, who prayed with us for God's will to be made clear to us. When JJ's retirement was finalized, we began looking for a house in Apple Valley, California. We did not move quickly because we wanted to be where God wanted us to be. But we felt that if this was not the will of God, He would tell us. God's will for our lives was very important to both of us, as God's direction had kept us under His protection throughout the past. We looked at many houses, chose several, but didn't feel God's agreement with them. We felt that this was not only retirement from work, but also retirement from the ministry. We really wanted to downsize since there was just the two of us.

God had other plans. We soon found a three-bedroom

house with a huge den and two bathrooms with an office attached to the garage. It was immediately known to us that this was the house that God wanted us to have. Everything went as planned. We moved into the new home, which was sixty-nine miles from Pastor Ken's church. This made it very difficult to be in service when the snow and ice blocked the freeway. So, I began to hold Bible study and prayer at home when we could not get down the hill to our church. Before we knew anything, others were coming to the bible study at the house, mostly people whom we had met during the meetings I had held in Victorville. I did not know where this would lead to, but I heard in my spirit these words, "I want you to bring to the High Desert what you have taken to the nations."

It was challenging to be used to the salary of a professional then to change to living on retirement, as none of the ministry expenses was ever paid for by anyone. Just us! So, JJ took a job as a security officer in Pasadena. The travel was so stressful that he only worked several days a week, and many days he would stay with our daughter, Jackie in Covina on the days when he was working. One night when I was alone. I had a dream or vision. I don't know which, but I saw myself and JJ in a huge room with baby cribs all over the place. JJ was walking around the perimeter of the room, which was brilliantly lit and sterile, not unlike a hospital's operating room. Soon I heard a knock at the door. When I went to the door, there stood a person whom I cannot describe. This person handed me a baby which I took. Then the person was no longer in front of me. I placed the baby in one of the cribs. Then there was another knock at the door. When I went to the door, there was the man holding another baby which he handed to me. Then he was no longer there. I took the baby and placed it in one of the cribs. This scene was repeated over and over again. As I looked at what had happened, I saw a room full of baby cribs with babies in them, and I began to care for the babies, changing, feeding, and holding them closely. I spoke to the Lord saying, "Lord these are not even my own children." At that saying, something warm and liquid began to flow from my heart, almost like a stream, into the babies. I knew that it was God's love pouring out of me into the babies. I looked around the room and saw JJ walking the perimeter or the room as if he was the overseer of what was happening in the room. I moved from one crib to another to make sure they were alright, and then came out of the vision. As I came out of this vision, I was somewhat puzzled. I did not want to tell anyone about it. But I could not forget it. In my heart I knew what the vision meant, even though I did not want to acknowledge or accept it. I didn't even tell JJ for a long while, and I did not try to interpret the meaning. I simply tried to put it out of my mind. After all I was considered a somewhat weird woman as worldly things did not impress me, nor anyone's opinion of my weirdness.

Because of the difficulty of getting to our church in Covina, we began to look for a church in the High Desert. Several Sundays a month we would visit a local church. I didn't realize that because of the intercessory prayer meetings I held and the bible study in Victorville, I was known by the pastors. Some of whom did not receive me well. So, we prayed and cried out to the Lord to help us find a local church. One night, after praying, I had a dream. JJ and I were climbing up a hill looking for a church. As we got to the top of the hill, there were several churches visible with groups of people in front of the buildings. They were waving to us to come to their building. As we were so impressed with their acceptable attitude, we started walking toward one of the buildings. I heard a voice speaking with authority, "Not them, this one." And my head turned towards a group of people who were standing together, not resembling a church. I knew it was God speaking to me, so I grabbed JJ's hand and started walking towards the people who did not look like a church. Again, I did not tell anyone about this vision. I didn't really know what it meant, since we were only looking for a church to attend. So, we stayed with Pastor Ken's church, attending when we were able to.

The group of people attending the Thursday night Bible study at our house increased. New people coming with the regular attendees. We began to have intercessory prayer on Tuesday nights. This group also increased in size. Most of these attendees were part of local churches, but were not attending regularly. I kept encouraging them to go to their churches on Sunday. Some did, but most did not. This lasted over two years. The thirty-two regular attendees began to call me their pastor. They wanted to give an offering at the Bible study but I would not receive one. I did not know where this was leading. If I had known, I would have run from it as I certainly did not seek this direction for my journey with the Lord.

In January of 1996, the Lord spoke to me and said that we were to do openly what we had been doing all along, which was to pastor the people. I knew that the call was on my life to pastor this church. So, when we acknowledged the call to establish a church, we found an auditorium in a local school in Apple Valley, Desert Knolls Grammar School. The Sunday service was to be held there although the first service was held at the Holiday Inn in Victorville on March 3, 1996, where Pastor Ken came to minister and to lay hands on JJ and myself. He also ordained JJ and me. It was a wonderful gathering with relatives, friends, and the faithful attendees there. The Spirit of the Lord was present in a great way, as Pastor Ken laid hands on JJ and me and we were slain in the Spirit. I arose knowing that God had called us to raise up this church for the people in the

High Desert. The move of God was evident throughout the process of getting approved by the state and federal government. When we were praying about the name of the new church, the name, Victory in Jesus came to me, but I cast it aside because when my Evangelistic ministry was registered, I tried to use that name, but it was already registered to some other ministry. But I could not move beyond the name Victory in Jesus. I was led to check with the Federal Government and the State of California. I was amazed when I was told that the name was free to be used. So, we knew that God's direction for the name of the church was to be Victory in Jesus. And of course, this church was going to be a Bible Faith Center. So, it is!

The first service at the school was held on March 10, 1996. With thirty-two people in attendance. There was a joyous presence of the Lord. Many of the attendees committed to being a part of the new church. It was an encouraging experience. One of the most exciting things was that my mother was a part of our church and was our first door greeter. Among the first members were Reggie and Jerry Hunt, who worked and supported me all the years of my pastorship. The Lord brought in a group of professional people who had political connections in the city of Apple Valley. As the congregation grew, their local connections helped us find a building that became our church residence. Many people helped to establish and convert the rented building into a house of the Lord. Our first service in the new building was well attended. Many of whom were new Christians. The church grew, with me as the pastor, and JJ as the assistant pastor. Surprisingly, this was accepted by our congregation. I can say without hesitating, there was in evidence a major presence of the Lord where healings and deliverance took place continually. I was not the instigator of God's movement there, the people's hunger and expectations. We had a greatly anointed praise team who all yielded their lives to the Lord as I demanded them to.

I led as the Lord directed me to, not as one trying to be like another church. Understand that I did not seek this position as I did not seek the position of the evangelist. But my obedience to the Lord is the major thing in my life. One thing that I knew nothing about was receiving a salary from the church. JJ had taken a part time job with the local phone company to help with the church's finances and our own. It was almost three years before we were asked by the board to please accept a salary. We agreed to accept seven hundred dollars a month. I admit that during this journey I have dragged my feet as the Lord revealed His direction for me to take, but it didn't take long for me to get on the path that He directed me. And since I knew nothing about pastoring, I continually sought the Lord for guidance. The major theme of Victory in Jesus Bible Faith Center's teaching was, commitment to and faith in God, obedience to His Word, being filled with and led by the Holy Spirit and reaching out to bring others to the Lord. I was in a place where I could see why the Lord led me in a certain direction as He continually guided me as pastor of the church. Our membership increased to two hundred and fifty. We had a packed house.

The church was committed to reaching out and touching lives. The Lord led us to establish outreach ministries. We were supportive to a ministry in Mexico operated by Rev. Anna Marie Espinoza. Each Christmas we would prepare gifts and food and groups of the members would travel to the annual Christmas celebration. At this service many people came from all over to receive their needs met. We developed a prison ministry, a ministry in the juvenile delinquent facility, an outreach ministry to children of prisoners, a ministry at convalescent Senior Centers, a youth ministry, and a weekly community outreach ministry. I felt that this was what this Church was developed for—reaching the lost and hurting, helping them to come to the Lord.

We continued to grow and serve the Lord. In 2005, one night as I was in my office preparing to teach the Bible study, I began to experience a pain in my chest and a shortness of breath. Having been a nurse, I had an idea of what this was, but I still got in the pulpit and taught without telling anyone what I was experiencing, not even JJ. After Bible study was over and we went home, my daughter Linda called me and I told her what I was experiencing. She said, "Mom, you need to go to emergency and get checked." JJ had become very disturbed because I resisted his insistence that I go to the hospital to be checked. He finally convinced me to go. He drove me to St Mary's emergency room and before I knew it, I was being admitted for having a heart attack. From there I was sent by ambulance to Scripts Hospital in San Diego where I was operated on for blockage of the heart. I was there for five days and sent home to recover. Within two week I was back in the pulpit. God is awesome!

The journey continued. In 2007 a piece of property a block away from the church was placed on the market. JJ and I sought the Lord about purchasing the property to build a church home for the increasing congregation. We were led by the Lord to do so, and the board was in agreement also. The churches Board of Directors were such a blessing. We could not have accomplished what we did without them. This was the moment that I knew that even when I didn't know the Lord, His plan was working in my life. I thought my going back to college to major in Agricultural Science was for our plan. Now I know that God knew that I would need knowledge of construction, reading plans, understanding State and county laws as far as building and maintaining property in the City and County was concerned. We searched for a construction company who was local and very committed to building a great house for God. By this time, JJ's health had deteriorated to the point that he was unable to be of any help with the process. I thank God for the congregation of the church who was there for me in the most difficult time of my life. I thank God for the knowledge hat I received in the college of His direction, where I learned how to read blueprints, to drive a tractor and all about concrete and foundations. At the time I couldn't understand why these classes were necessary in order to be a farmer. I know now that it was farming for souls that I was preparing for.

The building of the church took me in many areas that I had not experienced before. The first one was in seeking a loan for the financing of the Church. Although we had more than half of the cost in savings before I could sign a building contractor I had to get the financial matter settled. I incurred much prejudice doing this, not just racial, but anti-Christian policies in banking. Even the bank that held the church assets turned us down saying they did not finance church buildings. So, I had to go from one bank to another until I found one who had a manager who was a Christian and agreed to finance the building after we paid almost half with the churches savings. I moved the church account to this bank from the bank that refused us. Then the search began for an architect and a building contractor. After interviewing several, the one that we, (The Church Board of Directors) and I chose was an expert who had built several churches that he took me into to see his work. He began the plans showing me different kinds of structures. Through prayer, I had a drawing of what the building was to look like from the outside. It took several months to get the plans finished. While he was working on the drawing, he recommended a building contractor. After meeting with and praying about it, the Lord directed me to hire him. It was truly the Lord, as the whole process was to me a supernatural experience. I had to be on the building site almost every day. I thank the Lord for our Church Secretary, Linda Robinson who is now with the Lord. She was such a businesswoman with a gentle personality who was able to communicate with businesspeople and carry out God's direction without hesitation.

I must admit that this was a very difficult time for me as JJ was declining in health. But the Lord sustained me as I stayed totally connected to Him and His guidance. During the construction which took around nine months, I was working on getting the inside designed. The Lord brough help from many areas. My uncle's plumbing company, West Side Plumbing, based in Phoenix, Arizona came to do the plumbing. A member, Patsy Martinez son, Dominic Carlos's business did the decorative designing and construction of the inside. The building of the sound system was a donation by a local business. As the interior was being finished, the Lord directed me to buy Bibles and place them in the walls throughout the interior of the church, as this was to be a Bible Word teaching Church. As the work was finished and we were doing the outside planting and decorating the exterior, it seemed as if all my energy was depleted as we were preparing for the Church Dedication.

One evening, Pastor JJ and several men were planting trees outside as the women were working with me on the decoration, when Joseph Valery, a man that I had ministered the Holy Spirit to at Walnut Faith Center years ago walked in. I had not seen him in a long time, as he had pastored a church in Ontario, California some years ago. I was happy to see him as he said he was driving by when he saw JJ and the men outside planting trees and stopped to talk with them. He came inside to say hello. We talked awhile and as he was leaving, the Lord said, call him back and ask him to come and help you. I called to him, and he came back to me. I asked him what he was doing and where he was going to church. He told me, and I asked him if he would consider coming to be a part of our church, Victory in Jesus Bible Faith Center. He said he would pray about it. As he was almost at the door, he turned around, came back, and said I don't have pray about it, I will come and be with you. I was praising the Lord, as I knew that without JJ's help, it was going to be difficult for me to pastor the church. But God had a plan, and He was not caught unaware of what was going on in my journey.

The plans were all finished, and the church was completely decorated for the dedication. On November 22, 2009, there was a great dedication service with around three hundred attending. Our special speakers were Pastor Charles Harrell and Pastor Ken Clowdus. Also, the architect and contractor were present. I was so thankful for the opportunity to acknowledge those who had helped me arrive at this point of the journey that God had called me to. We were moving to the place that God had preordained the church to be. Pastor Joe Valery soon came on board beginning with overseeing the men's fellowship. We had always had a strong women's fellowship, as I was the head of this ministry, with retreats and conferences. After JJ's decline, the men's fellowship had several leaders, but did not grow as I had envisioned it to. Pastor Joe began to take them to a new spiritual level. He came on board the first of 2010. After a while, He began teaching our Thursday night Bible study. The members were very accepting of him. This gave me more time to spend with JJ as he was diagnosed with Alzheimer which advanced rapidly. This was devastating to me and our children. Even though they did not live in our community, we had a very close relationship with them. Their father was special to them.

As time went on, I was spending more and more time looking after him and having Pastor Joe as the assistant pastor was a real blessing. I knew that things would be changing, as the Lord began to prepare me. For JJ's safety and care, He led me to place him in a very special care facility, Sterling Commons in Victorville. It was not a facility for elderly people, but for specific care for those with Alzheimer. They cared for him, but we, my children and I made sure that he was cared for. After almost five years of Pastor Joe's presence at the church, the Lord said to give him the reigns, making him the Senior Pastor. I knew that this was coming, and I considered this as my retirement. I spoke this many times to the members, then the Lord said to me that this was not retirement, but refinement. I didn't know what He meant, so I just stayed in prayer as JJ's health declined. He was in and out of the hospital with other issues. Pastor Joe's ordination as the Senior Pastor of Victory in Jesus Bible Center was a very special time with Pastor Charles and Pastor Ken officiating. The congregation were very accepting to what God was doing. This gave me the time I needed to take care of the house and JJ.

As I continued along with my children looking after JJ's care, being with him daily, it was very difficult to watch this very special man deteriorate. One morning I received a call from Sterling Commons where he was being cared for. They told me to come as soon as possible as JJ was not responding. I called the kids and they prepared to come, and I went to the facility immediately. He did not respond to me or my voice. As I sat beside the bed, praying, and holding his hand, the kids came in. They were so devastated seeing their father, whom they loved so much, in this condition. We were there for around four hours when JJ's eyes opened. We thought that he was coming to. His eyes focused in one area and then they closed, and he was gone. I'm sure his eyes were on the angel who was there to escort him into the Kingdom of God. This was a part of the journey that I would loved to have altered. But God is in charge of the journey that I am on. This was very devastating as his passing on May 29, 2014, was only twenty days before our 62nd anniversary. This was a very sad time for us. He was such a wonderful husband, father, grandfather, and servant of the Lord. His interment was a military funeral with burial at Riverside Veteran Cemetery in Riverside, CA.

Before JJ passed, I had sold our big house with all the memories and purchased a small home in a senior housing community called Sun City. One thing I thank the Lord for was even before we became Christians, we were led to reinvest every bit of the money from the sale of our homes in the next house. We had purchased four homes when I moved into the house alone it was number five. There would be no house payment as the profit from the sale of the last house paid for my new house. Since I would be living on a very small budget, the Lord knew I would not be able to afford house payments. So, I rejoice in the fact that God knew I would be in this place at this time. This was a new path that I would be walking, and the sad part was that I would be walking alone. But God!

My time alone was the time that God manifested Himself to me in a comforting manner. On one Sunday morning at church, the praise was very anointed with Reggie Hunt leading the Praise Team, and the sadness that I felt was so great that I wanted to cry as we praised the Lord. Suddenly, I was in the Spirit, and my eyes opened to a scene that caused me to change from sadness to joy as I saw JJ standing before the throne of God with his arms lifted us praising God. I went out in the Spirit and ended up on the floor. This was my deliverance from the grief that was trying to hinder me from continuing the journey that God had before me. I was still over the Women's Fellowship at church. So, I was still ministering to them in their Monthly meetings and their annual Women's Retreat which was held in Palm Springs. It seemed as if this was a temporary situation as I did not have the feeling that I was in the place that God wanted me to occupy.

As I was ministering outside of our church more, the gift of prophesy was operating through me more and more. The interesting thing was that most of the words the Lord gave me had to do with things that were happening to fulfill words the Bible said would be taking place in the end time, to help them get ready. Many times, I would prepare to teach a sermon that had nothing to do with bible prophesy, and the night before the sermon, the Lord would lead me to change the message. I had learned over the years to follow the Lord's leading when He directs me in a different way to do things. The thing that caused me to seek God's direction was the word that I received from Him when I was questioning Him as to what I was to be doing now that I no longer was part of the church leadership. His word to me was that I was to prepare His people. I questioned Him as I said, "Lord isn't that what I have been doing all these years?" He revealed that as I was pastoring, it was as a teacher bringing a student from kindergarten to High School, but then going through college is where they are prepared for what's in their future. The Lord said you are to prepare people for their future which will be in heaven or hell. So, I understood that my call is to sound the alarm, to prepare people for what's coming.

Then the Lord directed me to the book of Jeremiah, to see what he had to go through when crying out for the people to hear what God was saying was going to take place and their need to be the people that God was requiring them to be to make it through the difficult days ahead. Some of my visions were overcoming, with no one to discuss them with, but to stay divinely connected to the Lord. Then He impressed upon me the scriptures in Jeremiah 1:4-9 *"Then the word of the Lord came unto me, saying, 5 'Before I formed thee in the belly, I knew thee; and before thou camest forth out of the womb I sanctified thee, and I ordained thee a prophet unto the nations.' 6 Then said I, 'Ah, Lord God! behold, I cannot speak: for I am a child.' 7 But the Lord said unto me, 'say not, I am a child: for thou shalt go to all that I shall send thee, and whatsoever I command thee thou shalt speak. 8 Be not afraid of their faces: for I am with thee to deliver thee, saith the Lord.'"* This journey is not an easy one. During what I call a training session with the Lord, He let me know that my call is not to prophesy to people about their lives and things they are encountering, but to Sound the alarm on His holy mountain. I understood that this was ministering to His people, and the Church.

The Lord led me to establish a ministry, God's Way of Victory, by which I would be able to operate according to the federal and state government standards. I began to hold a monthly meeting for God's women in a local hotel. The meeting is called God's Women of the Word (WOW). So, I am still on the journey the Lord began so many years ago. In the midst of all the personal difficulties, apart from JJ's passing, two years later my mother passed away, then my sister who was the first family member to accept the Lord went to be with the Lord. In the midst of political turmoil, racial violence, and church weakening and division, which was prophesied in God's word, now we have a Corona virus that was also prophesied in God's word. The isolation that is required is hindering God's church and the work of people like me. Now I understand that this is what I am to prepare God's people for, the end time calamities that will be permeating our nation and the world. To prepare them for the rapture of the church, to encourage then to make a choice, either it will be heaven or hell.

This is a time when we must choose who we will serve. Josh. 24:15, *"Choose you this day whom ye will serve."* The journey that God chose for me in the beginning has not changed although there have been detours and rerouting. I frequently ask the Lord, "Lord do you know how old I am?" Of course, He does. But my flesh has tried to shut down before the Lord was ready. In May 2019 at two o'clock in the morning, I had a heart attack. I knew what it was and chose not to contact my children or call for medical help. I said to the Lord, "If it's my time Lord, I'm ready." But God was not ready. Anyway, when I let the kids know about it, I ended up in the hospital for surgery to open up blocked arteries. Two weeks later, I was in Palm Springs hosting a Women's Prayer Retreat. I don't know when this journey is going to end, but I will be faithful to the call of God on my life as long as I am able. When I think of my mother and the call on her life, I recall that at one hundred years old she was on the phone praying with people who called her for prayer. I would like to be able to keep crying out to people to come to the Lord before life's journey is ended for them. That is what my call is at the end of my journey, to prepare God's people for the things that are before us according to the prophetic word of Almighty God. EVEN SO, COME LORD JESUS!

CPSIA information can be obtained
at www.ICGtesting.com
Printed in the USA
BVHW040157120422
634063BV00016B/236